HOW TO BE
A SUCCESSFUL
ILLUSTRATOR

A PRACTICAL GUIDE

RAY EVANS

Windsor Aug '87

Ray Evans

HOW TO BE A SUCCESSFUL ILLUSTRATOR

A PRACTICAL GUIDE

RAY EVANS

B.T. Batsford Ltd, London

To Angela, without whom this book could not have been written.

© Ray Evans 1993

First published 1993

British Library Cataloguing-in-Publication Data. A catalogue record for this book is available from the British Library.

ISBN 0 7134 6634 0

Typeset by Servis Filmsetting Ltd, Manchester
and printed in Singapore
for the publishers
B.T. Batsford Ltd
4 Fitzhardinge Street
London W1H 0AH

Page 2 Windsor Castle, 1987

CONTENTS

ACKNOWLEDGEMENTS

My special thanks go to Louise Simpson, who first conceived the book, to my editors Rosalind Dace and Jane Royston, and to Allan & Bertram Ltd, Royle's Publications Ltd and BP Chemicals Ltd, who kindly lent transparencies and original work for use in the book.

I would also like to thank the following for the use of individual illustrations: Allan & Bertram Ltd (pp. 45, 80–1, 82, 83, 84–5, 86–7); ATV (p. 67); BP Chemicals Ltd (pp. 40–1, 74–5); CCA Stationery (pp. 88–9); The Consumers' Association (pp. 46, 52, 54–5, 57, 59, 60–1, 84–5, 86–7); *Countryman* magazine (pp. 1, 38); *Daily Mirror* (p. 11); Eagle Star Insurance Group (p. 91); Foyle's Book Club (p. 50); HarperCollins Ltd (pp. 36, 47, 68–9); Innsacre Hotel (p. 76); *Man about Town* magazine (pp. 3, 10, 32); Merehurst Ltd (pp. 6, 48–9); John Murray (Publishers) Ltd (pp. 51, 64, 65); *New Scientist* magazine (p. 37); Procter & Gamble Ltd (pp. 78–9); *Punch* magazine (p. 32); Royle's Publications Ltd (pp. 27, 78–9, 92–3); Southern Gas Board (pp. 35, 95); *TV Times* magazine (p. 33); Van Nostrand Reinhold Ltd (p. 58).

All copyright holders and others whom I may not have been able to trace will be mentioned in future editions if the omission is advised.

Lastly, I would like to thank Andrew Lomax, who took the photograph of myself in my studio (p. 12), and Ronald Maddox for his excellent foreword.

Ray Evans RI, FSAI
Salisbury, 1992

FOREWORD

BY RONALD MADDOX PRI, FCSD, FSAI

ILLUSTRATION – SUCCESSFUL?

Illustration is a highly competitive field of art, covering all areas of publishing – books, magazines and newspapers – as well as displays and advertising for television, posters, record sleeves and other forms of promotional material.

Illustrators approach their work in many different ways. Whilst some artists are extremely versatile, others specialize, rather like actors, and become recognized and commissioned for particular subjects. There are some whose work is well-known. Illustrators are not accorded the same status as fine artists in Britain, as they are in some other countries, but a highly individual style often creates a demand and greater recognition.

Style surely means the illustrator's power of imparting to his work some quality of his own personality, and should not be confused with technique, although the latter is an integral part of style. Competent draughtsmanship alone is not enough. Two artists drawing the same subject, using the same basic materials, should at the end produce very different illustrations, because they will have implanted their own individuality into the work.

Given the ability to draw, there is no reason why a student cannot develop a particular style and technique, or an area of illustration which suits his or her special talent. An 'ability to draw' is a qualification which overrides many others, although in recent years it has often not been encouraged in many art colleges.

Drawing is something that may be cultivated by hard work and the opportunity to practise the craft, which was perhaps much easier in the days before the advent of the camera. Many great illustrators of the past developed their abilities through reportage, covering events which would nowadays appear as photographs in newspapers and magazines, or on television.

Some illustrators are able to express in a few simple lines what others take weeks to achieve. Cartoonists, for example, often have to work extremely fast, and have the additional challenge of being topical and witty. Other illustrators may have to produce meticulously accurate technical or scientific artwork, or even something that is all in the mind, such as space-fiction drawings.

The time factor – deadlines and an ability to meet them – has to become part of an illustrator's life, as does a good knowledge of art materials and equipment for working in either black and white or colour, to help achieve the right result and the tight schedules often imposed.

An understanding of printing and reproduction processes is extremely useful in order to prepare artwork that may be reproduced without problems, always providing that a printer takes trouble to get the best quality from the illustration.

Those who are already painters or printmakers may find this a very good basis for a career as an illustrator. These disciplines encourage observation in an artist, the use of sketchbooks, and the collection of material for future reference – as the forthcoming chapters will show.

This book covers the many and varied aspects of Ray Evans's work, and is intended to give professional guidance to the would-be illustrator. Reading and absorbing the contents should help to set students on the path which both he and I have followed towards a career in successful illustration.

Ronald Maddox PRI, FCSD, FSAI has had wide experience as an illustrator and designer, in addition to being a successful painter.

From a beginning as an art director in design and advertising, he progressed to private practice, working for many national and international clients and covering a wide variety of commissions from stamp design to large murals.

For some years he was Chairman of the illustrators' group of the Society of Industrial Artists and Designers (now the Chartered Society of Designers), and is currently on the jury for the Royal Society of Arts Students' Design Bursary Awards. He is also a Fellow of the Society of Architectural Illustrators.

Fig. 1 Pen-and-ink drawing of the Penniless Porch and Cathedral in Wells, Somerset

INTRODUCTION

I have been a freelance illustrator since 1950 and have had a surprising degree of success, especially in the last decade. In this book it is my intention to cover all the fields in which I have had experience, using my own illustrations as examples. I have worked in many different areas and for an extraordinary number of people, both as a cartoonist, and latterly as a book, magazine and advertising illustrator. These commissions have invariably led on to other things and I can honestly say I have never found the work dull or monotonous.

Within these pages I give advice to would-be illustrators with a little experience, on the threshold of their careers, in the hopes that I will provide ideas as a useful starting point. I discuss the work, methods and problems that I have used and encountered over the years, with descriptions and information that should be useful not only to the student but to the professional artist as well. In short, although there is no substitute for experience, I hope that by writing this book I will short-circuit many of the problems that could be encountered, and help artists benefit from my experience – hopefully enabling them to further their own careers.

There must be easier ways of earning a living than drawing, but there can be few more pleasurable. Yet illustration is not just a job, it's a lifestyle, and it is up to you, the artist, to create it. If you have a talent for drawing and an infinite capacity for hard work, as well as a pride in your achievements – plus the ability to bounce back after repeated rejections – then this is the career for you!

How to get into print is a catch-twenty-two situation. How do you obtain commissions when you have little or no published work to show? Whether you are a recent art-school graduate, or an amateur illustrator keen to make a career out of your hobby, in this book I will show you some of the ways in which you can make a living. I will also warn against problems which may arise, as well as giving a general idea of what illustration is all about.

Fig. 2 Cartoon drawn for *Man about town* magazine, 1957/8

When I was at art college, there was little information available on how to find work and make a living as an illustrator. I was luckier than most, as I had had eighteen months' experience in an architect's drawing office prior to art college, and I left college hoping to establish myself as a freelance illustrator straight away. However, I soon discovered that work experience would be a great advantage, so I joined a large advertising agency in London and stayed with them for six months. Gradually I took on more and more commissions in my spare time, until I felt that I had the ability and the confidence to try freelancing. Even then, I supplemented my earnings with part-time teaching work.

Whatever stage you have achieved to date – be it a student, accomplished amateur or a young professional – you must first prepare a portfolio. This should contain a comprehensive selection of your best work, including graphics and any printed material. It is also important to include a wide range of subjects: botanical illustration, figures, architecture, and so on. The wider the selection, the higher your chances of success will be, although you will of course have your own preferences and special abilities.

Once you have prepared your portfolio, start approaching local advertising agencies, design studios, publishers and printers. Addresses can be obtained from reference libraries by consulting books such as *The Writers' and Artists' Yearbook* (see the Bibliography on page 94) or by looking at your local telephone directory. Make appointments to see them and listen to what they say to you – even if it is harsh criticism! It is also useful to keep a watchful eye on the media. Study the wide range of magazines and publications currently available and the styles and types of illustration that are in demand. Cartoons, greetings cards,

children's and illustrated books and jackets, painting books, calendars, advertising and editorial illustration can all be studies for inspiration. Look at how your style fits in with these trends. It is important to study the market constantly and assess the ways in which your work can adapt to it. Never turn down the chance to try something different, and never stop learning how to express yourself in new ways. Even if you are not art-school trained, if you have the will-power and talent you will succeed.

You may find it necessary to obtain part- or full-time employment, as I did, to learn the basics of the profession and to understand how the commercial world operates before you decide upon freelancing. If this is difficult, submitting illustrations and paintings to art galleries is an excellent way of getting yourself known. Success here can lead to individual commissions, as well as offers of membership to illustration and painting societies. A well-respected gallery is a shop window on the art world and may create exciting and unexpected openings.

An agent will help to establish your work in the market place and direct you to useful clients, although this can be expensive. A good agent could take from thirty per cent upwards as a fee, and your work would have to be priced accordingly. However, valuable time can be saved by using an agent – time which could be put to good use in the studio. Exercise caution when approaching agents; do not be persuaded to pay out money to have your work reproduced in any way until you have researched the organization you intend to join.

Use your talents wisely and explore all avenues. As John Berger said in *The Guardian*, 'Talent doesn't necessarily mean facility, it is a kind of motor activity within a temperament – a form of energy . . .'

Fig. 3 'Sir John Smith, renowned meteorologist.' Cartoon drawn for the *Daily Mirror*, 1960

Fig. 4 A self-caricature, drawn whilst working on a television programme called 'A Box of Birds' in the 1960s. A similar portrait of one of my colleagues is shown on page 31

Chapter one
STUDIO EQUIPMENT AND MATERIALS

To start out as a beginner in illustration you will not need all the equipment listed in this chapter, but some items are essential, as you will soon discover. It may only be possible to acquire the more expensive items over several years, but you must have a minimum number of precision instruments, of which a wide variety are available. I will discuss the equipment that is indispensable in this chapter, even if you intend to be a cartoonist, or to concentrate solely on black-and-white work and feel that all that is needed is a pad of paper and a pen.

SETTING UP THE STUDIO

The first requirement is a room in which to work where you will be undisturbed and able to leave unfinished work in safety. This may well have to be an unused room in your house rather than a purpose-built studio like mine, but this will be quite adequate.

Fixtures and Fittings

Light
Good light is essential. A great deal of direct sunlight should be avoided, although blinds can be fitted if this cannot be helped, or if privacy is needed. The light source should come from the right or left, depending on whether you are left- or right-handed.

It is especially important to have good light for working at night. I do not like overhead strip lights, and have various spotlights in my studio that can be adjusted to points where I need light most; these are fitted with day-light-simulating bulbs. In addition, I have various adjustable lights that can be moved over the particular area in which I am working, the main one being screwed on to the corner of my adjustable base board. This type of light should be fully adjustable, both up and down and from left to right.

Work surface
A good bench or long table running under the light will be ideal. You will also need at least one good drawing-board, which should have a hard, straight edge for tee-square work. I made my own adjustable base board, on which I use various sizes of drawing-board at variable heights. Table easels can also be purchased, as can adjustable drawing-boards on stands.

Shelving and storage
You will need plenty of shelving. This should be conveniently situated on

Fig. 5 (opposite) The author at work in his studio

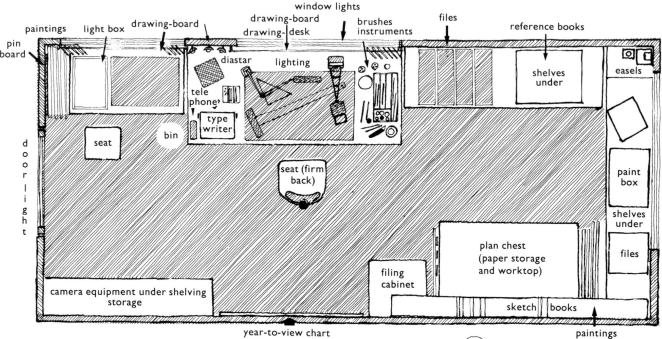

Fig. 6a A good basic layout for your studio

available wall space and used for storage of reference and sketchbooks, art materials and so on. If you have the space, storage cabinets for paints would also be invaluable.

Plan chests are obtainable from architectural suppliers, or you may find one advertised for sale second-hand in an architectural journal. These are essential for the safe storage of paper, board and artwork, and the top provides a useful surface for cutting or mounting work.

Office Equipment

I have found large pin boards indispensable for displaying urgent notes and messages, designs, roughs and wall charts, as well as a year-to-view calendar for quick reference. Other office equipment is as follows:

Telephone and answer machine

These are an essential part of your office equipment. A freelancer needs to be available to accept commissions and jobs as soon as the phone rings!

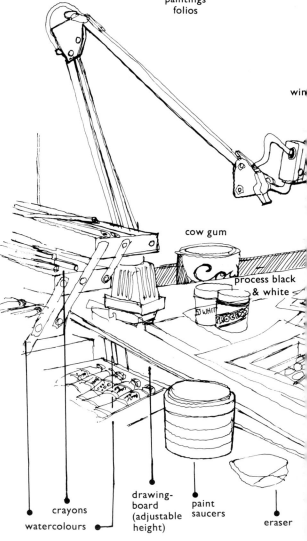

Typewriter/word processor

A word processor is an invaluable addition to your studio. Failing this, a typewriter will do as well, although this should if possible include a corrective facility to avoid frustration!

Light box/slide projector/magnifier

A good light box for viewing reference slides would be extremely useful (although not essential at first), as would a slide projector and magnifier. The magnifier should ideally be equipped with its own light.

Photocopier/fax machine

These are expensive pieces of equipment, and can certainly wait until you feel that you really need them (and, of course, you can afford them!) See also the section on using a photocopier on page 48.

Materials

The best possible materials are essential for good work, if you can afford them. This applies especially to the paper you will be working on.

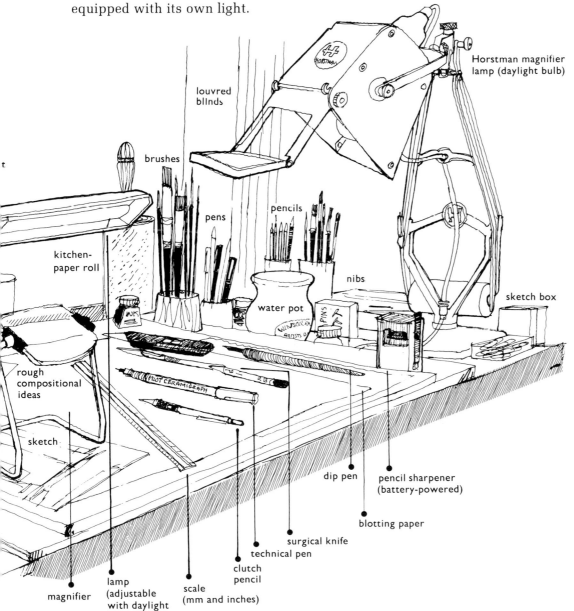

Fig. 6b A basic studio worktop with plenty of light

Paper

There are many different varieties of paper, and the type of illustration you are doing will dictate the sort of paper you use (see also page 64). If you are working on a fine illustration, then a smoother surface will be necessary, whereas a free-drawn, sketchy water-colour will require a rougher surface. Your local art shop or supplier should be able to advise you on the types of paper available.

I work mainly in pen and ink, or line and wash, and use a variety of papers for these techniques. For pen drawings I prefer a smooth, but not slippery, surface with a little 'bite'. This surface takes a pen or pencil beautifully and mistakes can be easily scratched out, with care, by using a scalpel blade. A good cartridge paper is one that takes a pen easily and does not bleed or fur. It should also be very white. The whiter the surface, the better the reproduction quality will be.

While using the line-and-wash technique, I have discovered that some watercolour papers, especially of the 'hot-pressed' variety, are very good for line drawing, but they are more expensive. Process white can be used for correction, but although it will reproduce perfectly, it sometimes spoils the effect of an original drawing. When working in colour I prefer a 'Not' or a 'hot-pressed' surface, but you may have a different preference.

I invariably stretch watercolour paper before working, which entails wetting both sides of the paper and sticking the edges down with gum strip. The drawing below illustrates the materials required, and the preparation of paper prior to drawing is described further on page 56. I keep up to half-a-dozen inexpensive boards, with paper often already stretched, for this purpose. I also like to wash out or blot my paper, particularly when beginning a watercolour illustration, and therefore do not use a surface that is too soft or absorbent. I am not keen on the harder hot-pressed surface either, as I find that the colour tends to slip about, and that there are no graduations in which the colour can lie, enabling texture to be produced by blotting or washing out.

Use paper of whatever weight you prefer, but remember not to use stiff board, as current reproduction methods require flexible paper to go round a drum. When in doubt over what surface to use, have to hand a small piece of paper on which to experiment. Otherwise you may waste a lot of time before discovering halfway through an illustration that the surface does not please you.

Fig. 7 Stretching watercolour paper using gum strip (see also page 56)

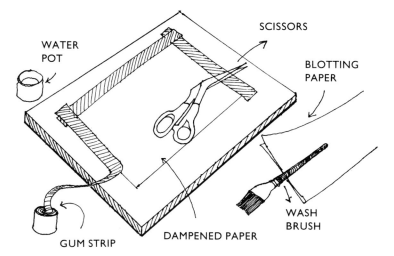

WATER POT

SCISSORS

BLOTTING PAPER

WASH BRUSH

DAMPENED PAPER

GUM STRIP

Pens

Pens are available from stationers and most art suppliers. I much prefer the water-based variety as they are odourless and do not 'bleed' through the paper.

Dip pens

For freehand drawing, the dip pen is unrivalled. Nibs are available in a variety of widths, and it is essential to have a holder that grips the nib securely so that you can make a firm stroke.

Clean your nibs frequently with paper towels or a cloth while you are working, and carefully scrape off dried ink with a scalpel blade. Make sure that the nibs are clean and dry when stored (they should be kept flat in a drawer or box), or they will rust. Always use good-quality Indian ink.

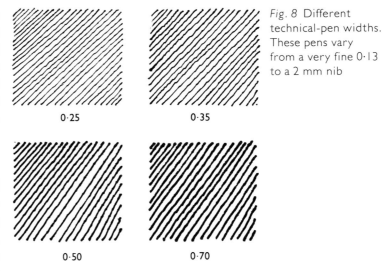

0·25   0·35

0·50   0·70

Fig. 8 Different technical-pen widths. These pens vary from a very fine 0·13 to a 2 mm nib

Fountain pens

Fountain pens are good for freehand drawing, but are generally not waterproof, which will be a problem if you intend to use watercolour or washes. These pens are available in a wide range of nib sizes, although you may need to shop around for a fine nib that suits you and is also flexible. A gold nib is especially good. If you do possess a good fountain pen, you will find that it is excellent both for sketching and for some freehand illustration.

Technical pens

Technical, or architect's, pens are necessary items, and are available in either refillable or throw-away forms. Sizes range from a very fine point (0·13 mm) upwards. The throw-away types last well and do not usually dry up, whereas refillable pens will dry up if they are not looked after carefully.

When using the refillable type, clean the pen out after use by removing the nib, emptying the ink container and washing it out with water or pen cleaner. The pen should be stored clean, dry and in a sealed container until next needed. This cleaning procedure is particularly important with very fine pens such as the 0·13 mm, 0·18 mm and the 0·25 mm.

This may all seem tedious, but these comments are based on experience and the fact that I have ruined dozens of pens in the past. I take care to look after my equipment, but sometimes, in the haste of a deadline, one does forget to clean pens properly, with dire consequences.

Fibre-tipped pens

There are many good felt- or fibre-tipped pens on the market in different thicknesses, and these are useful for layout and field work. Rolling-ball pens are also excellent for drawing, and some makes have the added advantage of being waterproof. As well as the finer-tipped pens, you will also need a good, broad-line, square-tipped pen, preferably water-based and waterproof. If you choose spirit pens, make sure that you are using bleed-proof paper, and keep caps firmly screwed on when not in use.

Pencils

I use a variety of clutch pencils with HB, B and 2B leads in 0·3 mm or 0·5 mm thicknesses. These are clean and easy to use, and therefore ideal for artwork. Ordinary lead pencils, however, take some beating, and I use these regularly (see pages 67–9). The hardness of the pencil depends on the proportion of graphite to clay in the composition of the lead, and is denoted by a B (soft) or H (hard) number. Degrees of hardness range from 9B to 10H.

I also have a battery-operated pencil sharpener conveniently situated at my elbow. (A sharp knife or craft knife will do the job even better, if not as quickly.)

Coloured pencils

Coloured and watercolour pencils are used for line work, colour shading and hatching, and come in very handy for colour roughs (such as those shown on pages 52, 77 and 88). Traditional, wood-cased colour pencils come in three types: (a) those with heavy, soft-coloured leads which wear down quickly; (b) those with finer, non-crumbly leads most generally suitable for illustrative work; and (c) those with leads made of water-soluble colour, which can be spread into controlled brushmarks or washes with a paint-brush. Water-soluble colour comes in

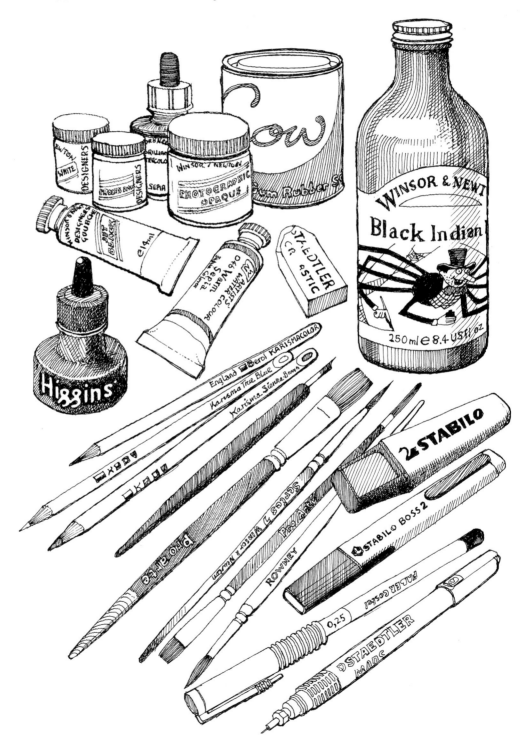

Fig. 9 An assortment of the pens, paints and inks that I use regularly in my work

useful where subtle blending is needed, although overlaid hatched strokes of different colours can also be used to create a textured effect. Coloured leads are also available for some types of clutch pencils.

Paints

I mainly use Winsor and Newton watercolours in my work, but there are occasions when other media are needed to achieve particular effects.

Watercolour, gouache and acrylics

I prefer watercolour tubes to pans, but whatever your choice, and whichever medium you are using, you should always buy the best paints that you can afford. There is a range of very good acrylics on the market, and again, what you choose will be a matter of personal preference.

Different media require different approaches. Gouache, for instance, should never be used too thickly as it tends to crack when dry. Acrylics do not crack when used thickly, but they only come in a limited range of colours which tend to be rather crude. Nevertheless, brilliant results are possible with acrylics, and I know many artists and illustrators who use them to great effect. I only use these colours thinly, as I do watercolour, so that they retain an attractive transparent quality.

I tend to use the minimum number of colours for artwork which is to be reproduced, as the reproduction will be truer to the original. Even a six-colour process (see page 24) will find it difficult to reproduce your work accurately if you use several different primary colours, while greens made from two or three different blues – and the blues themselves – will confuse the camera.

The basic colours that I use are Raw Sienna, Brown Madder Alizarin, Olive Green, Prussian Blue, Warm Sepia, Rose Doré, Antwerp Blue, Scarlet Lake and Ivory Black. Sometimes, in the field, I will take only Brown Madder Alizarin, Prussian Blue, Raw Sienna, black, a tube of gouache white if I am working on coloured paper and a few collapsible brushes.

In the studio, I use, in addition to the above, Burnt Sienna, Cadmium Red, Permanent Rose, Winsor Red, Chrome Orange, Permanent Magenta, New Gamboge and Indigo. Some purists may question the absence of a colour such as Ultramarine. Again, this is a matter of personal preference – I do not like Ultramarine as a colour, although it does make excellent greens. Prussian Blue and Alizarin are very strong colours, which may not appeal to some artists, but I particularly like the effects that these can give.

Some colours are more fugitive than others. All colours will fade gradually in sunlight, but for illustration purposes this does not really matter. Most of the colours listed here come in the cheaper range, although some of the most interesting paints come in the more expensive bracket, including Cadmium Red, Permanent Magenta, Permanent Rose and Rose Doré. However, I would never use all these colours in one painting!

Whatever your range of colours, you will choose at first by trial and error, but soon they will begin to put a stamp of individuality on your work. Lastly, for studio work you will need process white and process black.

If you intend to specialize in botanical or medical illustration, there are reasons for using pure colour, and as many colours as you can collect. The mixing of colours can otherwise be very painstaking where it is vital to reproduce the colour of the original object precisely. Liquid watercolours are the answer for this type of work.

A final word or two about preparing artwork. You should always stretch the paper, protecting the painting area by using masking tape (see page 56). Work with a clean sheet of blotting paper under your hand, working across or down depending on whether you are right- or left-handed, and away from areas already painted.

Brushes

The watercolour brush is probably the most important tool that an illustrator uses, and the care and attention lavished on it are therefore very important. The best brush for general use is, in my opinion, a fine sable (Winsor and Newton Series 7), which, with care, should last a lifetime. Sable brushes hold a good quantity of colour and yet maintain a very fine point, providing they are looked after. For my present work I tend to use sable brushes in the smaller sizes (from 000 to 3), and synthetic brushes in the larger sizes. There are excellent brushes in the synthetic range, and I have regularly bought the square-ended variety of synthetic or nylon brush to use in my architectural paintings. My favourite size of large-wash synthetic brush is $1\frac{1}{2}$ inches.

While in use, keep your brushes standing in a jar or similar container with the handle at the base to protect the points from damage (Fig. 10). Always wash and dry out brushes when you have finished with them. New brushes, or those not in use, should be kept in a closed and dry cabinet or drawer. When using acrylics, particular care must be taken to wash out every vestige of colour. Never use brushes with masking fluid: I use an architect's ruling pen for fine lines, and, when opened, large areas can be laid with the side of the pen. If a brush does become clogged, use warm water and soap to wash it out.

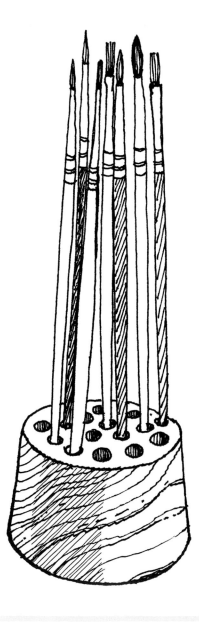

Fig. 10 You can buy a simple wooden brush holder, or make one by drilling holes in a block of wood

Airbrush

If you are interested in becoming a technical illustrator, an airbrush will be a useful piece of equipment. Some of my colleagues are experts with the airbrush, although I have never liked its rather mechanical effects for the type of work I do. Those who specialize in the more technical side of illustration often do the most exciting and clever work with this tool. For the same kind of effect I splatter with an ink nib, or get textural feel by flicking the end of a small stencil brush dipped in colour. Paper towels, tissue paper, sponges, blotting paper and masking fluid are all useful alternatives.

Inks

There are very good Indian inks available in a wide range of colours. One point to bear in mind is that, if you are using ink colour or washes, the ink you choose must be waterproof. You must also remember that, with the exception of black, process white and process black, inks do tend to fade if exposed to bright sunlight.

Miscellaneous

There are numerous other materials that you will need to accumulate in order to carry out illustrative work. The following will provide a useful checklist:

- racks for paints and brushes
- assorted waterpots and jars
- pot palettes for mixing colours
- saucers (not plastic)
- French curves
- transparent and heavy metal rulers
- tee square and set square
- cutting tools (scalpels, Stanley knives and blades)
- scraper-board equipment
- dry-transfer lettering
- reference books and sketchbooks in various sizes
- photographic reference
- masking fluids
- process black and white
- sharp scissors
- erasers
- pencil sharpener (preferably automatic)
- gum strip
- drafting tape and sellotape
- absorbent paper

Field equipment

Finally, you will need several items for field work. Watercolour sketching boxes, brush cases and bags for sketchbooks are essentials. A collapsible seat should at least be kept in your car, and taken with you when a lot of field work is anticipated.

You will also need a good camera with a close-focus lens, in order to take slides either for your reference or for agents and clients. A second, compact camera is also very useful for field work.

WYCOMBE HOUSE
HIGH WYCOMBE FURNITURE
MANUFACTURERS SOCIETY
CAR PARK AT REAR

Chapter two

DRAWING AND PAINTING FOR PUBLICATION

After approaching advertising agencies, publishers and so on, you should start receiving your first commissions. In this chapter I will give you basic guidelines about what to expect, and information on facts of which you need to be aware before you embark on your career as a freelance artist. If you wish to explore these areas further, there are many good books available on these subjects (see the Bibliography on page 94).

COMMISSIONS

With each commission you receive, there are certain things that must come first, one of which is to establish the price for your work. If you have an agent the price must include his or her commission and also VAT if you are registered (see also pages 48–9). Agents will work this out for you. Otherwise, this is often the most difficult part of the job, as your client will obviously want the best price he or she can get. (This does not always apply with long-standing clients, when they are familiar with your prices.) If you are unsure of how much to charge, ask an experienced artist or consult an illustrators' society.

Do not undercut your colleagues or you will disrupt the current market rates, but do not be greedy either. You will learn with experience the rates that you should be charging, and you should always be able to come to a satisfactory agreement.

Many book and magazine publishers have fixed prices for book jackets or illustrations, but often you can negotiate a price. Consider the time you will take for the work, whether or not expenses are included, and the cost of your materials. You should see the client yourself, and find out whether preliminary 'rough' artwork is part of the agreed price. It is as well to charge separately for roughs, and you should make clear at the start that this charge will be payable even if the client decides not to go ahead. An advance is fairly essential in many cases and this also proves good will.

When calculating your rates, remember that each job is different. I am not really in favour of charging on an hourly-rate basis, because as you become more experienced, it is this expertise that the client is paying for, which cannot be rated on an hourly basis. Another factor is that the more experienced you are, the quicker you will be at arriving at the correct conclusions and producing good roughs. Finally, ascertain the date for the finished artwork. More information is given on commissions later in this book in Chapter Five (see pages 46–9).

Fig. 11 (opposite) An on-site watercolour sketch of a house in High Wycombe, made as a preliminary to the finished studio painting for a Victorian calendar. Finished size approx. 8 × 9½ ins

COPYRIGHT

Again, if you have an agent, he or she may handle details such as copyright, but in most cases you will be dealing directly with the client. In my experience is it better to meet them before commencing work to find out whether there are any problems regarding copyright. If you are using artwork which has already been published by another client, they will require an acknowledgement and your new client will require their written consent.

You should read up about copyright for yourself, but the basic rule is never to copy the work of a living artist, nor that of an artist who has been dead for less than fifty years. Once the fifty years have passed, copyright is no longer applicable and the work becomes freely available to those who wish to use it. Copyright infringement is not generally a serious difficulty – except perhaps with recognizable faces or figures – but cartoonists and caricaturists are in a good position because of the great exaggeration that is used. Certainly, well-known places and architecture can be copied freely, except that you should never copy slavishly unless requested to do so. If you can visit the site yourself, make drawings and take your own photographs, so much the better.

Copyright on your own work belongs to you in all cases, unless you have assigned it to someone else in writing. If the latter, this should be for a specific use only, unless you sell the rights as a whole.

JOB DETAILS

Obtain a written brief from the client in advance. Details should include whether the artwork is required in line, halftone (line and wash), line with one or two colours, or in full colour.

When you are producing work for publication it helps to know how many colours are used in the printing process. As many as six colours may be used, although normally there are only four: cyan, magenta, yellow and black. Printing-ink colours are somewhat different from the colours you will be using, and subtle differences will be apparent in the result. Pantone markers will enable you to match printing-ink colours while working on a commission. Remember that if you are using two different blues or reds, for example, it will be difficult for the printer to match your colour work exactly if he or she is using a four-colour process. You should therefore mix from the three primary colours and black, although with a six-colour process less care need be taken.

PAPER

Always use flexible paper or card if work is to be printed. This is because, in the lithographic process, artwork is bent around a rotating drum to be scanned before colour plates are made.

It is as well that you know the surface and weight of the paper on which your work is to be printed. With a newsprint or cheaper type of paper, make sure that you draw with clean, firm lines, using cross-hatching to 'shade' (see Figs. 15 and 16 on page 29), and avoid large areas of solid black.

REDUCTION

Too much reduction will make cross-hatched lines fill in, as line work spreads on the cheaper type of paper, so firm, solid drawing is needed if reduction is to be used. However, if the work is to be reproduced on good-quality fine-art paper or smooth, hard paper, fine lines and washes can be used and the work will stand greater reduction. With black-and-white work or pencil drawing I prefer to work the same size (S/S) as the finished illustration will be, or not more than a third up, although some reduction can actually sharpen a drawing.

With most work, even in colour, a reduction of more than half is to be avoided. Some reduction, however, is unavoidable at times, particularly with book illustrations where some work has to be reduced because of sheer lack of space.

Look at the diagram I have drawn to illustrate this point (Fig. 12). Draw a rectangle the actual size of the drawing when reduced, then draw a diagonal from the left-hand bottom corner up through the top right-hand corner. Continue this line, and a rectangle now drawn on this diagonal will reduce or enlarge in the same proportion to the size the work will be printed (see also pages 53–6). The figures shown are the fraction of the enlargement.

REFERENCE

For all types of illustration you will often need reference, and you should build up your own neatly filed reference library so that it is easy to turn out the material you need. I have built up a photographic library over the years and have a cabinet for this purpose, although this takes up considerable space and needs constant revision and weeding out. A good public library can also be very useful.

Sometimes you will be asked to draw from fairly minimal reference. I have often worked from small photographs where a good deal of embellishment and imagination are required. These commissions have usually been for travel books, hotel guides and some calendar illustrations. The drawings for the hotel and travel guides are shown in Chapter Five.

It is, of course, much better to work from an actual subject or building. Where book illustration is concerned and you have a story to illustrate, you will probably have more time to obtain references or visit sites, or to use your imagination after carefully reading the book.

Fig. 12 Diagram illustrating the technique of enlarging or reducing on the diagonal

USE OF TINTS

With a black-and-white drawing on which you wish a mechanical tint to be laid, you can colour the area with blue, or outline with a blue crayon. The colour-separation process is not blind to blue, but monochrome line and halftone are. A mechanical tint such as letratone may also be used, and cartoons can benefit from this method, which I use for some of my work. I think it better to draw your own cross-hatching (see Figs. 15 and 16 on page 29), but this is a matter of personal preference. Study catalogues for tints and other drawing aids.

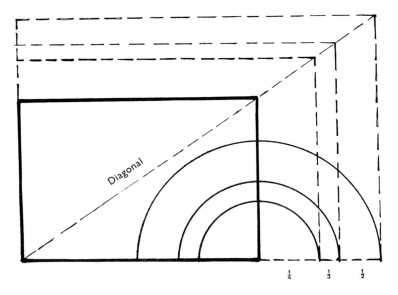

Fig. 13 Watercolour sketch of Troutbeck, for a studio painting of the same subject used in a 1992 Victorian Calendar. Finished size approx. 9 × 9 ins

My own sketchbooks form very useful reference and I have shelves of those that I have filled over the years. When using reference, try to draw freely with a pen or pencil, as though you are drawing *in situ*, so that the spontaneity shows through. If a careful pencil-drawing outline has to be made first, draw quickly and freely over it with the pen. There are some very good books on pen drawing which may be helpful (see the Bibliography on page 94). When introducing a second flat colour it is a good idea to draw it in black on an overlay, along with a colour sample or a pantone number.

Ray Evans.

PRESENTATION

Whether you are sending or presenting roughs, finished roughs or finished artwork, make sure that you present your work cleanly and attractively. There is nothing more off-putting for a

COTTAGE in foothills
Mountains of Mourne
NORTHERN IRELAND
Ray Evans
These houses seem to grow out of the ground

client than to receive scruffy artwork. Perhaps when you are famous you can get away with it, but you certainly cannot when you are a beginner! I work under the maxim that I always present my work attractively, even to long-standing clients. Put your sample work in plastic sheets, preferably in a ring binder or in folders where it is protected by film or sleeves. Always be neat and tidy, even with the smallest commission. If you are not delivering the work in person, ensure that it is well packed and sent by registered post or recorded delivery. You should also insure it against damage.

Finally, be professional at all times — even with clients you know well — and never trust the 'I'll see you all right' client! Take a pride in your work, and always do the best you can. Remember, the better your rough artwork, the more chance you will have of a good result and also the less work you will have to do at a later stage (see, for example, my finished roughs on pages 52, 77 and 90). This is particularly important when you are a beginner or if you are working for the first time with a new client.

Fig. 14 Calendar illustration of a cottage in Northern Ireland, drawn from photographic reference

Chapter three

CARTOONS, CARICATURES AND PEN DRAWING

The cartoon world has been a very happy hunting ground for me. My early success was totally unexpected, but I was lucky in that when I left college in the early 1950s there were dozens of newspapers and magazines vying for the public eye, as this was the period before television took over. I have a feeling that we are returning to a similar situation today, as more people become disenchanted with what television has to offer. Magazines are increasing in popularity, particularly in specialist fields, and newspapers are thriving.

I had no knowledge of how to set about making a living using drawing skills when I left college. Fortunately a neighbour who was a successful cartoonist and writer encouraged me by saying, 'You have a natural sense of humour and you can draw'. I decided to discover whether he was right, and I sent my work to *Punch* magazine. A year later, after sending in six drawings a week (three hundred in total!), I sold them my first cartoon.

regularly published cartoons, and sent them my work. Any drawings which were rejected were sent to others. These were finished drawings in pen and ink: it is no use sending roughly drawn ideas when you first start out, although this may be feasible at a later stage when an art editor is aware of your abilities.

It is vital to study the market. My main targets at first were daily newspapers and popular magazines, of which there are many more today. You only have to look at the *Writers' and Artists' Year Book* to see lists of them! There are also numerous technical and specialist publications, including scientific, building, engineering, sport, computer and commercial magazines. Many contain cartoons as well as humorous and serious commercial illustration (which I will discuss further in Chapter Four). Once you have researched your market, study the type of humour the newspaper or magazine would be most likely to employ so that you can focus on that aspect.

NEWSPAPERS AND MAGAZINES

At this time I began to make frequent sales of my cartoons to newspapers and magazines. During that first year after college I selected several which

STUDYING THE MARKET

As well as studying the illustrations in this book, it is worthwhile studying the work of wood engravers; look at the work of other cartoonists and illustrators in books, as well as magazines and newspapers, and try to discover their technique. Why is it that artists have different styles of their own, as distinctive as any trade mark, and easily recognizable without seeing the signature? Try to see what it is that makes these artists different from each other. You will gradually develop your own style of drawing, but don't try to exaggerate this too soon – let it develop naturally.

CARTOONING

Many of the cartoon ideas I see today are funny and apt, but the drawing sometimes offends me. This is not because the cartoons are lacking in detail – some artists can be brilliant with the merest lines – but because they seem carelessly drawn. The cartoon illustration in books and annuals dating back to the 1930s and beyond was very good and often highly detailed. Do not attempt to draw as these artists did, but study them and learn from them, looking at how they worked. Every artist develops a style – although it may take years to emerge fully – and it will be a contemporary style, the style of today. My own style has changed and developed considerably during my career.

PEN AND INK

Nearly all cartoons and caricatures are carried out in black and white, so it seems appropriate to include here some instruction on the use of pen and ink. Look at Figs. 15 and 16 and practise making marks on paper. Try to create tones, curves and perspective, and use these techniques in your drawings. Practise with a dip pen and black drawing ink (this should be the waterproof variety). Experiment with different paper surfaces: you will find that your line will change or be affected by the paper surface you draw on. Try

Figs. 15 and 16 (below) Cross-hatched lines drawn with dip pens may be used to create a variety of tonal effects

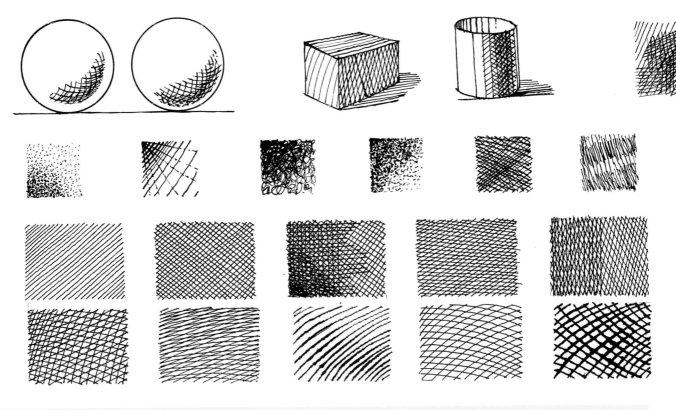

using paler inks and washes, or mixing darker and paler inks together. Newsprint paper, however, still needs a bold black-and-white approach, and it is important to remember that there is nothing like a pure, dense black line, combined with solid black areas.

Splatter ink with the end of your finger; experiment with broad and fine, hard and soft nibs; and try using a quill. When drawing in line, vary the thickness by applying different pressures. It is also useful, as I have already mentioned, to study the work of wood engravers to see how they achieve their results. I was lucky enough to learn something of this art, and the discipline required for engraving helped my pen line considerably.

Technical pens are good because they are so convenient and easy to use, particularly when making quick sketches in public places. Although they lack the sensitivity of the nib pen, they can be used to create beautiful drawings. Try fountain pens too; a well-known cartoonist friend of mine rarely uses anything else. However, non-waterproof ink must be used in fountain pens, so you will not be able to use a wash or watercolours with them. There are good coloured inks on the market, but they do tend to fade more

than black ink. Some felt pens will also fade from black to brown, as will watercolour, in strong sunlight.

Drawing figures

Draughtsmanship is an important skill and can take years of practice to master. Do not be afraid of hard, repetitive work: whether you are interested in illustrating children's books, drawing cartoons or entering the more serious commercial market, you need to be able to draw well. In many cases your drawing will not have to be highly detailed, as simple line drawings can sometimes be extremely effective. Sophisticated reproduction processes mean that line work can be reproduced very well, but remember that, if the drawing is reduced too much, some of the quality of the line will be lost.

Style, pattern and design are an important part of your illustrations. First you have the idea, and then you have to draw the picture and compose the figure or figures. If you look at old magazines, you will see that the cartoons were extremely well-drawn and quite complicated in detail. Figures were not usually distorted and exaggerated as they are today, and the humour lay in the caption, rather than the drawing. Today the drawings themselves are much funnier, and sometimes – particularly in the case of political cartoonists – extraordinarily drawn and exaggerated in a style reminiscent of Hogarth and Gilroy. It is worthwhile studying these artists, who lampooned politicians and royalty alike.

Fig. 18 shows the figure of a man in a box. Look at how I have made him fit the shape. Drawing a border, or shape, around the image forces the artist into designing within this area. Try various shapes – rectangles, circles or ovals – and then create drawings to fit them. It

Fig. 17 Interesting effects may be obtained by masking out areas of paper and flicking on colour with a stencil brush

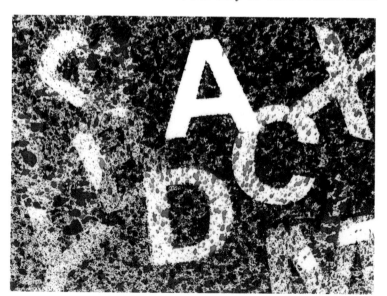

is good fun and you can learn from the exercise. Draw the lines out in pencil first, then ink in the outlines afterwards when the picture is as you want it. Rub out the pencil marks, then gradually complete the drawing with hatching, or solid blacks. If you are nervous about how the hatching will look, practise on a spare piece of paper, or complete the hatching in pencil first.

If you wish to improve your figure drawing, I would recommend joining a life-drawing class. If you are not already attending an art college, you will find these classes at your local adult-education centre, or at local colleges or schools. It is invaluable to learn how the figure is constructed, and life classes can help enormously.

Fig. 18 Working within the confines of a pre-drawn rectangle is a very useful discipline for design

Cartoon humour

I have now arrived at the difficult part – how to produce the funny idea. It is, after all, the idea that sells, and I have sprinkled this text with what I used to sell as funny ideas. The caricature of a bird (Fig 19) is of a woman with whom I worked on a television programme called *A Box of Birds* some years ago. I used photographic reference and thumbnail sketches, and made a careful likeness of the subject before giving her a bird body. I drew similar caricatures of all those involved on the programme, including myself (see Fig. 4 on page 11).

To capture a likeness is something of a knack and takes practice, so try first on friends or members of your family. Try drawing direct: many artists find that they can do this, and it is a skill that will improve over time. If you have difficulty with this method, take close-up photographs and use them for reference. When trying to think of a funny idea, choose a familiar subject and the ideas should begin to flow. The interesting thing about comic art is the

way one idea leads to another – life itself is often very funny. Try to be topical and up-to-date with your illustrations.

Make rough sketches of your best ideas, so that you do not forget them, and carry a small sketchbook with you at all times, so that if an idea materializes or you hear something while travelling or going about your daily business, you can make an instant note of it. Remember to make your finished drawings somewhat larger than they will appear in print, so that if there are any details or lettering they can be easily read.

The first drawing that I sold to *Punch* magazine was of a monk sitting at a desk with a large scroll manuscript spilling about him on to the floor. He had drawn a huge capital letter full of decorations and intertwining details, but was scratching his head with his quill, obviously at a loss as to what to do next. You might think this not immediately funny, but a great deal depends on the quality of the drawing. This particular cartoon happened to tickle the fancy of the art editor that

Fig. 19 A caricature of one of my female colleagues, drawn whilst working on a television programme called 'A Box of Birds' in the 1960s

Fig. 20 Cartoon drawn for *Man about Town* magazine, 1950s

morning when it arrived on his desk, but don't forget that there will be hundreds of other drawings for him or her to look at too. Once I had started, ideas for more cartoons containing monks began to flow, such as the monk riding a scooter with its illuminated 'L' plate (Fig. 20). Other ideas showed a monk on a scooter with a stained-glass windshield, and a monk gliding along with roller skates peeping from under his habit, with his superior looking on suspiciously. You are probably ahead of me with ecclesiastical jokes by now!

At about this time I sold a series of mechanical-men cartoons to *Punch*, which appealed to other editors too (an example is shown in Fig. 21). These were old ideas adapted into a mechanical age – try to think this way with other subjects. If you study cartoons from different sources you will see how easily ideas spring to mind and create further ideas.

As you gain in experience you will soon learn what amuses different art editors. Do not send less than half-a-dozen of your best cartoons at a time. Put them in a strong envelope with protective backing and enclose the same-sized envelope stamped and

Fig. 21 (right) One of a series of mechanical-men cartoons drawn for *Punch* magazine, 1950s

addressed to yourself. This is most important or you will not get them back. Don't be put off by rejection slips: I collected them for a while by the dozen.

Cartoons with captions

When producing cartoons with captions, the caption must be pithy, to the point, and as short as possible. Some cartoons contain words within the drawing, such as the Indian rope trick (Fig. 22). Of all the ideas in this chapter, I particularly like the French-horn cartoon (Fig. 23). It is terribly obvious, but the best puns usually are. My puns have in the past caused me to be threatened by members of my family, until they are pretty well banned!

Strip cartoons

I have not been involved a great deal with strip cartooning, although I drew a weekly character for a children's magazine once where I had to work weeks ahead and always had to draw

Ray Evans

Fig. 22 (left) Cartoon drawn for the *Daily Sketch*, 1958

series of strips before sending them off. Better still, go to see an editor or agent, or test your idea out on friends and colleagues. Strip cartoons appear in children's annuals, bumper-fun books, comic annuals, puzzle and game books, books, magazines and newspapers — look at all of these and decide where your forté lies. Lastly, decide whether you wish to use your own name or a pseudonym, and then establish your style of writing it.

By now, you should be able to see how my mind works, and this should help you to get into your own way of thinking so that you can create your own methods and techniques. Later on, as you will see, my serious drawings became very different from these early cartoons and humorous illustrations when I changed course and gave up this sort of work. Study the work of our leading cartoonists and caricaturists such as Ronald Searle, Gerald Scarfe, Giles, Ralph Steadman and Trog. Look at a good book in the library covering the last fifty years of illustration: it is interesting to see artists' different approaches over the years. Never try to copy directly. You must evolve your own way of drawing, but you can still learn a great deal from the work of others.

the same character, as is often the case when illustrating stories. This continuity is important: an illustrator must be able to repeat characters in a strip cartoon so that they are recognizable in many different positions and guises, and this takes practice. Strip cartoons are often used as a serious feature in specialist magazines, such as how to construct a cloche in a gardening magazine or how to build furniture. Study such magazines carefully and see what openings there are in these areas.

If you have a series of good ideas which you feel might make a strip cartoon, draw the strip somewhat larger than it will reproduce so that the lettering can be read easily. Draw it in black ink, with balloons if necessary, and draw in the wording carefully and clearly. You will need to practise this lettering until you have a clear and good-looking style. Complete a whole

Ray Evans

Fig. 23 'He's no Viking — those horns are French.' Cartoon drawn for *TV Times* magazine

Chapter four

DECORATIVE AND EDITORIAL ILLUSTRATION

With any form of illustration, from designing postage stamps to creating book jackets, the aim of the artist is to embellish, describe and make an impact on the eye of the beholder. Humorous and decorative illustration are closely allied to cartooning, and also to editorial illustration for magazines, where the text and illustration are closely linked.

HUMOROUS AND DECORATIVE ILLUSTRATION

As I concentrated in my early career on cartooning, much of my published work was of this nature and editors saw me as a humorous illustrator.

Consequently I began to illustrate for magazines already using my cartoons, and one newspaper started to send me other people's ideas which they wanted me to draw, either because they were not well-drawn or were just good ideas without a drawing. Such are the ways in which work can develop.

I also found myself being asked to illustrate articles and create humorous editorial headings. Once you know what the subject is, be it fishing or farming, it is fairly easy to think of something humorous to go with it, such as the 'Angler's Arms' sign with the hand extension (Fig. 24). These kinds of illustrations are meant as design fillers, to help the page look more attractive and to add interest.

EDITORIAL ILLUSTRATION

I really enjoy being asked to fill in on articles with pithy ideas. Look at the chapter heading for the *Guide to Food in London* (Fig. 25). The picture of mermaids with chips may be corny, but it appealed to the editor, which was all that mattered. I hope that you are now with me in appreciating that an odd sort of mind is needed to be a humorous illustrator, but you will find that this comes more and more easily with practice. With decorative work, it is

Fig. 24 Cartoon drawn for *Country Fair* magazine, 1956

Ray Evans

Fig. 25 Column heading for article entitled 'A guide to food in London', *Country Fair* magazine, 1950s

Figs. 26a and b (below left and below) Illustrations drawn for the Southern Gas Board's training booklets on public relations and how to use the telephone

important to remember that you are making a comment as well as embellishing the page.

Trade magazines

At about this time I drew a number of editorial illustrations for trade magazines. These publications are always on the look-out for cartoons and illustrations, and if you are a beginner and work for a firm that produces such a magazine, you can do no better than to start there.

My work appealed to the editor of a range of magazines for the Southern Gas Board, and shown here are two of the drawings I made for him to illustrate information booklets produced by the company (another can be seen on page 95). The illustrations had several functions: to get across a message simply in an amusing way; to be easily understandable; and of course to enliven the text. I was given the text for a small booklet on public relations, which I had to illustrate with humorous drawings (Fig. 26a). The idea was to convey the more serious aspect of public relations in a lively way, and I hope that the drawings did help. Another similar job for Southern Gas involved a company training booklet on how to use the telephone, which I designed and illustrated. The illustrations were comical ideas suggested by the chapter titles, so that they emphasized the points being made in a self-explanatory way (Fig. 26b).

Decorative illustration

The humorous and serious often overlap in this way, as in a book that I illustrated called *The London Cookbook*. The majority of the illustrations were straightforward drawings of London scenes, but many were small, humorous 'fillers' such as the one shown in Fig. 27 (overleaf). These were intended to break up the typescript and give variety to the look of the page,

Fig. 27 Column breakers in a book which I illustrated entitled *The London Cookbook*

and come in useful for filling odd gaps when a book is being designed. This particular book had four different categories of illustration: humorous fillers and line breakers; decorative illustrations on the title and chapter-title pages, filling the whole page and incorporating the text heading (Fig. 28); full-page illustrations; and lastly the cover, which showed scenes of London. This book was a joy to do as I visited the sites with the author, and we discussed all the illustrations at length. Such an author/illustrator relationship is

Fig. 28 Chapter-heading illustration for *The London Cookbook*

unhappily all too rare, and you will find that it is not the general rule, although in advertising work there tends to be more contact with the client. This is always helpful and you should endeavour to make personal contact for discussion and an exchange of ideas whenever possible.

Specialist magazines

The drawings shown opposite (Figs. 29a–c) were for an article requiring precise and diagrammatic illustration. They are decorative but convey a strong message about the commercial problems of town planning, the design of motorways and sewage disposal. They are realistic diagrams and their purpose was to explain in an eye-catching way, which is really the essence of what this kind of illustration is all about.

Most illustrators, in time, become specialists in a particular area or areas. Some work in fairly narrow but highly skilled fields such as botanical or medical illustration, developing their skill to such an extent that they become indispensable (provided of course that there is enough work available). Others may concentrate on figure drawing, editorial illustration for magazines or strip cartooning.

I myself have done a fair amount of general illustration, especially in the early years when I moved from cartooning into television and more general work, and you can see from this book the variety of work that I have covered. As I spent so long training in architecture and in drawing skills before going to art college, however, my interest in architecture has made me specialize more and more in this direction. As your work becomes better-known in a particular field, the result is that more work in similar areas will be offered, until eventually there will seem little time for anything else!

At the beginning, however, you will have to diversify and be prepared to tackle whatever you are asked to do – provided you do not get too far out of your depth. This can result in unsatisfactory work, which may do more harm than good to your career prospects. There will be times when you wish you could withdraw work that you have done in the past, so be careful not to get led into uninteresting commissions that have little future. The wolf has to be kept from the door, but do keep your standards up. Hack work in advertising – such as drawing uninteresting furniture – has to be done by somebody (and I did it myself in the very early days), but it is poorly paid on a local level. Technical drawing for advertising is quite different, however, and is often highly skilled and, most importantly, well-paid.

When you have had some success and gained some experience, try to join a society such as the Society of Architectural Illustrators or the Society of Illustrators and Designers (see *The Writers' and Artists' Year Book* for other societies).

The only real way to learn is by practice. A musician cannot carry on his or her career without hours of practice each day, and if you are not prepared to do the same, you may as well give up the idea of a career in illustration. Drawing constantly is the finest discipline and is great fun, and if that too becomes a chore, then you really are in the wrong career. If you are to succeed, you must literally live and breathe drawing. The opportunities for editorial work are immense – new specialist magazines appear on the bookshelves almost daily, and the scope for illustrators in this field grows apace. As always, study your market well, and you may be surprised at how much this type of work has to offer.

Fig. 29a–c
Illustrations for a specialist-magazine article on various aspects of town planning

a) Motorway costs

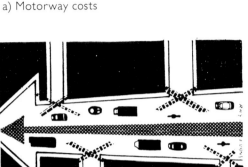

b) Road closure

c) An introduction to sewage treatment

Ray Evan S

Gelli, Cahel C
curig.

Home of Evan Roberts
the botanist
Gelli
Cahel Curig 15/7.

Chapter five

ARCHITECTURE AND TRAVEL

This chapter concerns my two favourite subjects. They go together well because, although I love to travel anywhere, the most fascinating places for me are where the architecture is really worth seeing and studying. The beach may be tempting, but the interesting city wins every time. I have been to many cities in Europe, the USA, many of the Arab countries and Thailand, and the wealth of different architectural styles is amazing. This chapter also links up with my discussion of advertising and calendar illustration (Chapter Eight), as much of my work in those fields has also had an architectural or travel element.

From the days when, as an 18-year-old articled pupil in an architect's office in North Wales, I stumbled around old cottages taking measurements in a surveyor's notebook, returning to the office and making accurate $\frac{1}{8}$-inch-scale plans and elevations, I have been fascinated by drawing and painting buildings. In those early days of making measured drawings we used theodolites for taking levels. Later, in the army in North Africa and Italy, this knowledge was very useful when I joined a Survey Regiment.

Working from observation posts, I would make two identical drawings of the enemy front – often high up on mountains or at the top of church towers. We used fixed theodolite bino-culars (transported by mule and later by jeep), and the drawings would be made with a super-imposed grid. These had vertical and horizontal degrees, with towns, villages and enemy positions (if known) marked. One copy went back to the HQ operations truck and I had only to give readings in degrees for them to pinpoint the area in which I had seen enemy movement or gun flashes. Any cross-bearings were noted and targets fixed for the artillery. In this rather unusual way, I performed my first commissioned illustrations.

Some of the work I am required to do has to be done on the spot and S/S (same size). Other work may be carried out in the studio from sketches made on site, and the third kind have to be drawn from photographic reference supplied by the client.

WORKING ON THE SPOT

I will be dealing further with 'measuring' on pages 43–4, but first I will take you through the initial preparation of a drawing made in situ. For this I use a variety of hardbacked sketchbooks, from the smallest at 133×102 mm ($5\frac{3}{4} \times 4$ ins) to 250 mm (10 ins) square. These usually contain paper of 140 lb (300 gsm) weight for working in the field or travelling. When on specific

Fig. 30 (opposite) Pen-and-wash drawing made on the spot of the home of the late Evan Roberts, Welsh naturalist and old friend of my father's. The drawing took about an hour to complete. It was used to accompany an article about returning to my past, written by my wife and published in *The Countryman*

Fig. 31 Watercolour made on-site in Cleveland, Ohio, in the USA. One of three watercolours commissioned as a BP limited-edition print. Finished size approx. 12 × 16 ins

Palace Square & the Old Stone Church.
Cleveland. OHIO. 3/5/90.

commissions I use watercolour blocks of 410 × 310 mm (16 × 12 ins), and 140 lb (300 gsm) in weight with a 'Not' or a hot-pressed surface.

It is best to be comfortable and to have a good folding seat with a back rest if you will be drawing for one or two hours. Sometimes I have to make do without a seat and, if the weather is bad, to get out of the rain!

The important factors to consider when working *in situ* are proportion, scale and perspective.

Proportion

Medieval and Renaissance painters made a grid to position the subject in front of them, with a grid of the same proportion on the paper or canvas. I put up a 'mental' grid when I am looking at a subject, and it is useful to cut a card with an aperture of the proportion to which you will draw, rather like looking through a camera viewfinder.

I spend at least ten minutes looking hard at my subject and getting to know it, and using my pencil for rule of thumb (see page 44) to gauge the width of the windows and the spaces between them as well as their heights in proportion to the whole height of the building. These proportions must be correct whatever building you are working on – Victorian or Georgian, medieval or modern.

It is important before you begin to ascertain what size the features such as windows are going to be on the paper and to check your viewfinder. There is nothing more annoying than to discover that, having started at the top, your building is dropping off the bottom or side of the paper. This has happened to me more than once, and I have even seen work by a very well-known artist with a piece of extra paper tacked on the bottom of the page (when you are famous you can get away with it!)

When working on site I do not make a preliminary drawing, but start directly with a pen if it is to be a black-and-white drawing. In this way the work is kept lively, whereas using ink over pencil will make for a stilted drawing. Other artists may disagree, but that is the way I work. It is a technique that will need practice, so if you are not confident enough for this, draw just a few guidelines in pencil first. Sometimes, if working in colour, I begin directly with a brush (usually square-ended), leaving spaces for windows and doors. With the main areas coloured in, I work with a pen, correcting the colour work where necessary; then back to colour, and then to pen again. This makes for a free drawing, and if the colour and line do not always tally this can be quite attractive.

Scale and perspective

Scale can be accurately assessed by introducing the known height of an object, such as a vehicle or a post box, or, ideally, figures. Establish your eye level with a pencil line at the beginning of the drawing, and the human heads will be at approximately this level (unless of course they are seated, going up or down steps or are children). The heads will therefore all be at the same level, but figures in the foreground will be larger with their feet and legs lower down the paper, and the other figures will get smaller the further they are away from you. Note here the painting of the Brandenburg Gate in Berlin (Fig. 59b on pages 78–9), which is a good example of perspective using figures.

If your viewpoint is high up, the figures will get smaller as they recede. However, the heads will not be at eye level, except those at the top of the

picture (see the small watercolour of Marrakesh market in Morocco (Fig. 32).

The easiest way to check perspective is to use a plastic ruler held horizontally at eye level. As buildings recede, lines above eye level will slope downwards, and those below will appear to slope upwards towards eye level. Vanishing points will differ according to whether buildings are parallel to you and each other, or not. Careful observation will make perspective more easily understood using this simple method. If you wish to study perspective in greater depth, I would recommend that you read *Anatomy, Perspective and Composition* (see the Bibliography on page 94).

Measuring

As with all specialist subjects, you must have a good knowledge and understanding of architecture in order to be able to draw or paint it. Although the process of drawing is fundamentally the same whether you are drawing buildings, people or bowls of fruit, architectural drawing demands a clear vision and the ability to assess accurately the proportion of one part of the subject in relation to another.

'Measuring' is one method that artists have always used to accomplish this. We have all seen the stereotype of the artist with one eye shut, holding a pencil out in front of him and waggling his hand from the vertical to the horizontal. I have even used this well-known figure as an idea for one of my cartoons (see Fig. 2 on page 10). Like all stereotypes, this image has, of course, a degree of truth in its outward appearance. What is being portrayed is 'measuring', and if carried out correctly this can be an indispensable aid for assessing proportion.

Fig. 32 Watercolour painting from a café above the famous market square in Place Djemmaa El Fnaa, Marrakesh

Fig. 33a I made this pen-and-ink drawing of the centre of Chester on-site, and made additional detailed colour notes for the subsequent studio painting

Fig. 33b (opposite) The finished painting, used as an illustration for a *Royal Britain* calendar published by Allan and Bertram, 1990

To explain, let me take Fig. 33a as an example and describe the process in relation to this sketch of the main street and clock tower in Chester (the finished painting is shown opposite). Having drawn the central archway and stonework that spans the road, the next step was to draw the wrought-iron clock tower. But how tall should it be? I put out my arm, holding the pen vertically, and shut one eye. Lining up the top of the clock-tower roof with the end of the pen nib, I slid my thumb down the pen holder until my nail lined up with the base of the tower (at the feet of the figure standing on the walkway).

This gave me one tower measure which, by moving my arm (still held out straight) around the subject, enabled me to find another object of the same apparent size. By a process of trial and error I found that the width of the main

archway from near to inner edge was exactly the same as my tower measure. What I needed to remember, therefore, was not how tall it appeared on my pen but this relationship between the two features – in other words, that the apparent height of the tower is the same as the apparent width of the main archway (not including the depth of the arch). As I had already drawn in the main arch, I was then able to measure that width on my drawing.

This time, I placed the pen on the actual drawing, with the tip of the nib on one side of the arch and my thumb-nail on the other side. A step of this distance above the walkway positioned the top of the clock-tower roof.

You will notice that I have used the term *apparent* size, for that is what you need to assess: the proportion of one object against another not as they are in actuality, but as they *appear* to be from our particular viewpoint. Take, for instance, the third post from the left in Fig. 33a. It is the same apparent size as the distance from the walkway to the centre of the clock, or from the edge of the Chester Grosvenor sign to the wall.

By this process, measuring can be used to assess the relative proportion of one part of your subject against any other part. There is, of course, no need to use measuring all the time, but it can be an extremely helpful aid in discovering mistakes if and when a drawing starts to go wrong.

WORKING IN THE STUDIO

When carrying out studio paintings I stretch 140 lb (300 gsm) paper to the required size, masking the picture area on my board (see page 56). I work most often S/S or slightly larger, but always in proportion to the finished reproduction size. I draw a grid on the prepared

surface using a tee square and set square. They are not necessarily equidistant, but these horizontal and vertical guidelines will help my free-drawn architectural composition.

I then make a drawing that is quite carefully finished, working lightly in pencil, and when I am satisfied with the composition, proportion and perspective I am ready to paint. I have enough experience to begin work straight away, but it may help if you work out your composition first on another piece of paper before launching into the finished painting.

USING PHOTOGRAPHIC REFERENCE

If I have only photographic reference for a painting, I will hopefully have more than one photograph from which to work; otherwise I will have sketches, drawings and photographs of my own. I invariably carry a camera to photograph the subject, including close-ups of detail that perhaps I was not close

enough to show properly in my sketches. I may also have had to make closer studies in addition to my main study. Photographs of figures can also be useful, and although I usually stay fairly close to my original painting on the spot, any additional information will be useful when I come to make my studio painting. When I am sketching figures, I like to look at them in groups so that they make shapes and patterns, and to paint them like this.

Working entirely from reference photographs is not easy and requires a lot of experience, particularly as far as imagination and invention are concerned. Photographs flatten the subject, and I like to make free-drawn interpretations just as if I were viewing the same scene for myself. It can be useful to have any photographs blown up in size on a colour laser copier.

TRAVEL COMMISSIONS

It has sometimes been a habit of mine to illustrate my letters with drawings, and it was this that gave me an interesting commission to illustrate a hotel guide. I had written to the editor of the guide because there was an error on one of their maps, and at the top of my letter I illustrated a small watercolour of a hotel which appeared in their guide to France. The editor then invited me to illustrate his annual book, which I did for nearly ten years. Occasionally I visited a hotel where I was able to use a drawing made on the spot, but mostly this work entailed drawing from photographs.

My job was to illustrate the hotel, and, if necessary, to flatter it a little. I also adopted the idea of using my own hand-drawn lettering to give cohesion to the chapter-headings for each country. The work was sometimes taxing, but always enjoyable.

Fig. 34 This illustration demonstrates the role played by figures in establishing the size relationship of different features in a drawing or painting

The skill in drawing an architectural subject such as a hotel is to make the drawing into an interesting pattern whilst emphasizing the most important features, which are invariably the roof line, the windows and the doors. The introduction of figures, or a car or two, not only helps to bring the subject alive but gives a much-needed sense of scale to the drawing. As an example of this, cover the fishermen in Fig. 34 with your figure and see how the boats and buildings immediately lose their size relationship.

The type of illustration used for the hotel guides is very different from the colour diagram I have shown of our house in Winchester (Fig. 35), which reveals the architectural details and building construction of the house. If you intend to draw architecture you must study the construction of buildings – I have found time spent undertaking such research of immense value for subsequent work.

The drawings that I made to illustrate the Consumers' Association *Guide to Italy* (see Figs. 39–43 on pages 52–7) are different again. These drawings are decorative, and are intended to embellish the page as well as to illustrate the subject. These were carried out from photographic reference plus some imagination and reference drawings of my own. As I know Italy well I enjoyed illustrating this book very much, and subsequently designed the third-edition cover, which is shown on pages 59–61.

When sketching a subject on the spot, I have often found that it is not always easy to make the finished picture, completed back in the studio, as lively as the sketch. Sometimes the actual painting can be carried out on the spot, but often a client wishes the building to be depicted at a different time of year or at an angle that cannot be seen directly, so photographs are usually necessary as well as sketches.

Fig. 35 Watercolour illustration of the author's former house in Winchester. This was painted as an instructional diagram showing architectural features for my *Drawing and Painting Architecture* book (published by Van Nostrand Reinhold)

USING A PHOTOCOPIER

I have often been asked to carry out black-and-white and/or coloured work for a letterhead, business card or brochure – or all three. For the colour work, life is made easier today by photocopiers, which can be used to reproduce line drawings exactly in order to colour them up. If you don't have your own photocopier, every town high street will have at least one shop offering this facility. Most machines will accept paper of up to A3 size, although there are some more specialized photocopiers that will take up to A1 size (you will probably need to telephone around your local area to find one).

You will need a machine that can copy on to various thicknesses of paper – take along your own watercolour paper and have the line drawing copied on to it. A hot-pressed surface is best for this, as the image will break down on a surface with too much texture. The paper can then be stretched and prepared in the usual manner (see page 56). Be sure to avoid rubbing the image while the paper is wet, however, as this can remove some of the photocopying ink.

I recently illustrated a book on Wessex, which entailed some interesting driving around Wiltshire, Somerset, Dorset and Devon illustrating the various regions. Some drawings were for chapter headings (to go at the top of the page over the title) and I chose long, narrow subjects for this purpose (Fig. 36). There were also spot drawings to go in the text, some of which were full-page illustrations, for which I used a fountain pen and a dip pen. This was a most enjoyable commission, and it is always good to be given the opportunity to search out your own subjects to suit each chapter.

EXPENSES

It is reasonable to expect some travel expenses on this type of commission, and this can be a separate arrangement or part of your contract for the work. If you are registered for VAT, it is more advantageous to have a separate arrangement for travel, particularly abroad where air fares are concerned. Your subsistence when abroad will not be VAT-rated, and nor will travel by train or air.

If you charge expenses, money that you receive for subsistence is taxable in Britain. This money can be reclaimed, or an easier option would be to charge the amount directly to your client if this is possible. Do not forget to

add VAT to any commission you receive, but do not add VAT to your expenses. An accountant may be helpful in explaining what the tax office considers to be viable expenses.

If you are self-employed and paying Schedule-D tax, you will have to prove that you are a *bona fide* practising artist and that you are receiving income before you can charge expenses (your accountant will help you here). As with any commission, be sure to establish your terms before you begin the work, and if possible, obtain a written contract. By law, the contract does not have to be a written document – your verbal acceptance of the commission is a contract, as long as it contains the three elements of an offer, a consideration (payment) and an acceptance.

The trouble with a verbal contract is that it is obviously open to misunderstanding, but to help avoid the pitfalls there are now model contracts which you the illustrator can send to the commissioning agent stating your terms and conditions. The whole area can be very complex, and I would recommend that you read *Rights*, a guide to contract law (published by the Association of Illustrators).

One final note on architecture and travel. When you are drawing buildings, you should ensure that you are not trespassing, and if you are in doubt, ask permission. This will invariably be granted, but owners like to be asked, and can often provide you with useful information (such as relevant dates) about your subject.

Fig. 36 Chapter-heading illustration for a book about travelling in the Wessex region of south-west England

Lightly
Poached

Lillian Beckwith

Chapter six

BOOK-JACKET DESIGN

Apart from the author's name (if he or she is well-known) the cover of a book is its strongest selling point, and this is why a professional illustrator will be paid much more for designing a jacket than for individual illustrations within the book. More work and experience are needed to design a book jacket, and, in addition, you will almost certainly be working in colour, whereas illustrations on text pages are more often in black and white. Prices for the latter are usually assessed on whether they are full-page, half-page or spot drawings.

The primary function of a book jacket is to stand out amongst the countless others filling the shelves of every bookshop. The jacket is the publisher's own shop window, so they will be prepared to pay well for a good, professional piece of work. This does not mean that the jacket should have a loud and violently conveyed message: that depends much more on what the book is about and to whom it is meant to appeal. The British, sadly, are not a great reading nation like, for example, the Russians, many of whom – from all classes – read books at every opportunity, even while walking the streets. In one respect, however, the British are avid readers, and that is if we are children, or buying books for children. There we can match almost anybody in a rich field of illustrated books.

Although I have illustrated books for teenage children, I have not designed book jackets for the very youngest end of the market where the best and more exciting books may be found. A friend of mine who illustrates books for small children writes them as well, and this is probably a very good way of going about it. There are some good prospects in children's-book illustration, but you must study your market well and have some pretty good specimens in your portfolio before approaching a publisher or agent who specializes in this particular field.

If, early in your career, you are commissioned to design a jacket, you

Fig. 37 (opposite) Watercolour jacket illustration

Fig. 38 (left) Jacket illustration for *The Lighthouse Boy*, a Scottish adventure story (published by John Murray)

Fig. 39 Finished crayon rough, drawn on detail paper, for a book-jacket design for *The Holiday Which? Guide to Italy* (see overleaf for finished artwork)

will have to work very hard on it. The first and most important task is to read the book carefully, and then to ask the author if he or she has any preferred passages in the book or whether they would prefer to leave the decision to you. When working on a jacket I start with some small, rough ideas for my own benefit, and when I have decided on three alternatives, I carry them out the same size as they will appear on the jacket, working on detail or layout paper in coloured pencil. These crayon roughs should be drawn carefully to give the client a good idea of how the finished work will look. The reason that I do my roughs on detail paper – and I would suggest that you do the same – is so that the client can physically wrap them around a book to get a

good visual impression. If you are new to the client, he or she may wish to see a finished rough (perhaps in watercolour or gouache if this is the medium in which you will be working) before asking for the finished artwork.

I have shown a number of different designs here dealing with fiction and travel (having specialized myself in the latter), and I will take you through one design, showing each stage of work through to the finished jacket. I have shown one of my finished crayon roughs (Fig. 39), as well as the finished artwork (Fig. 41, overleaf) and two versions of the printed jacket (Figs. 43a and b, page 57).

There are three main considerations in producing jacket artwork: the subject, the medium and the design. The

example that I have chosen was for *The Holiday Which? Guide to Italy.* I originally drew all the black-and-white illustrations for this book, and this was the third cover that I had completed. Having illustrated many jackets for this client over the years we understand each other very well, which makes things much easier!

For this particular design I chose southern Italy, and designed three different roughs. One reason for using this subject was that I had made several watercolour sketches there on a previous trip, and even had a drawing of the church tower that I sketched as a young soldier in 1943! This made it possible to have first-hand material from which to work, which is always an advantage, as well as additional photographic reference.

The positioning and style of the lettering and its background are of primary importance in the design of a book jacket (see also pages 57–8). In this case, I altered the positioning of the lettering from previous years' designs to fit in with my new layout (the main emphasis of the design being on the right rather than the left), and I dropped the quotation to the lower half of the design.

I sent the three roughs to the editor, who returned them having made his choice (Fig. 39). He gave me an accurate size in millimetres (mm) and asked for a large 'bleed' of 8 mm all round, as the design was to be a 'wrap around', covering the whole cover: front, spine and back (Fig. 40a). This was to allow for trimming the design and providing enough overlay for fitting the lettering and the whole design to the cover. This 'bleed' is very important. If the design were to be for the front cover and spine only, there would be bleed at the bottom, top and right-hand side. The left-hand side would then finish on the left edge of the spine with *no* bleed (Fig. 40b). In Fig. 41 you will see how I

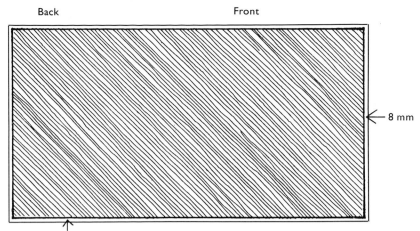

Back   Front

← 8 mm

Area of 'bleed' on a wrap-around jacket

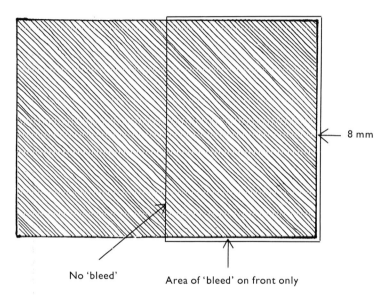

← 8 mm

No 'bleed'   Area of 'bleed' on front only

left room for all the lettering to fit, and where I left sky behind the main title and faded the colour so that the lettering on the spine could be seen. The same applied to the left side of the back cover, where some information about the book would appear. My intention was for the title and spine to show up particularly well when the book was on the bookshelf.

It was then time to start on the finished artwork (Fig. 41, overleaf). I used a 140 lb (300 gsm) watercolour paper, which I had stretched ready for use. I left room to make a drawing about a third up on the finished size of the book, which was to be 110 × 260 mm (the vertical measurement always

Fig. 40a (top) Diagram showing how artwork should be presented, with the correct 'bleed' for a wrap-around jacket design

Fig. 40b (above) Diagram showing the 'bleed' necessary for the front and spine only of a jacket

Fig. 41 The finished artwork for *The Holiday Which? Guide to Italy*

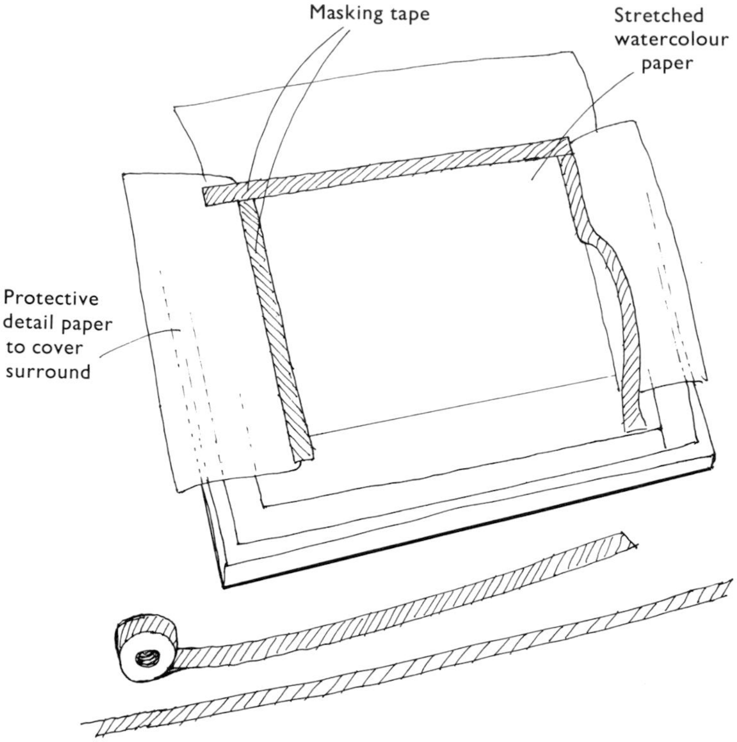

Masking tape

Stretched
watercolour
paper

Protective
detail paper
to cover
surround

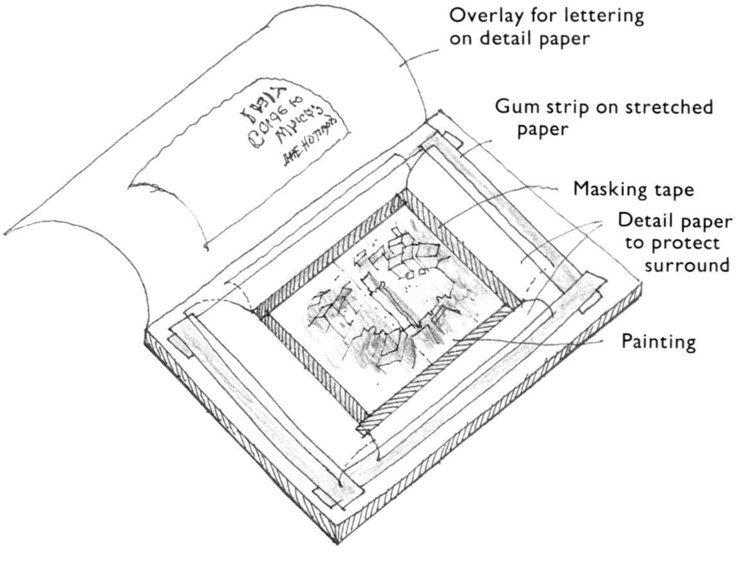

Overlay for lettering
on detail paper

Gum strip on stretched
paper

Masking tape

Detail paper
to protect
surround

Painting

Fig. 42a (top)
Diagram showing
the use of masking
tape to protect the
edges of artwork

Fig. 42b (above)
When the masking
tape is removed you
will be left with a
nice clean line
around the
illustration

drew a vertical line until it cut the diagonal, and, using the tee square, I drew a horizontal line across from this latter point until it hit the vertical line drawn up from the left-hand base corner. I now had a new, larger rectangle exactly one third up on the final book size, and drew an 8 mm bleed line around that rectangle (Fig. 40a).

At this stage I put four strips of detail paper, about three inches wide, to one side – these were to protect the surrounds of the drawing. I cut four pieces of masking tape long enough to go along each side of my rectangle with an inch or two to spare. I pressed the tape down on another board, running my finger over it to remove some of the stickiness from the gum side to make removal easier when the design was finished. I placed the strips of detail paper so that they were parallel to each side of my rectangle but half an inch away. I then stuck my inch-wide masking tape down firmly, exactly flush with the lines of my rectangle and overlapping the strips of detail paper, thus protecting the surrounds of the paper (Figs. 42a and b).

Next, I worked out the size of my lettering (which was to be one third up on the finished size) on a sheet of detail paper taped to fall over the design. With my lettering all placed, I traced the outlines lightly through, using graphite tracing paper, on to the prepared watercolour paper.

If you follow this procedure, the design can then be drawn in pencil so that you know where the lettering will fall. I always draw the finished drawing directly on to the paper until I am ready to paint it. If you feel that you are not experienced enough to do this, work on detail paper until you have the drawing as you want it, and then, using the tracing paper, transfer it on to your prepared surface.

The painting could now be started. I worked with flat colour washes, first

comes first). Carefully using a tee square and a set square, and working to the left lower side of my drawing-board but leaving several inches to spare from the edge of the stretched paper, I set up this size in pencil as a rectangle, and then drew a diagonal from the left-hand bottom corner up through the top right-hand corner. I then continued the base line to one third its length again. From this point I

blotting slightly until the main colour surface was complete, before gradually working in the detail with brushes, adding shadows and darks where necessary, until the design was finished. Sometimes I use a pen to sharpen the lines, but in this case I used only brushes.

With the design completed and quite dry, I removed the masking tape slowly, using a hairdryer to soften the gum so that it peeled off easily without tearing the paper underneath (see Fig. 50 on page 65). If there is any slight tearing of the surface, you can repair it by rubbing down gently with a bone handle, but if you take care to remove the masking tape slowly, this should not happen. If there is any slight bleeding of paint that has crept under the tape, use process white sparingly, if a scalpel will not remove it.

An interesting development with this design came some months later, when the format of the Consumers' Association jacket designs were changed to include the title wording in a panel. The tower was obscured, and was shown instead on the spine. This necessitated the artwork being returned to me to extend the sky and cliff some two inches above the top of the design. Fortunately there was enough paper around the original artwork for me to do this. Although there was not a great deal to do, the actual painting required some skill so that the join did not show. An extra fee was negotiated easily as they were old clients, and you can see the resultant jacket (Fig. 43b) along with the original design (Fig. 43a).

The other book-jacket designs in this chapter show the variety of my work, but you will surely come up with many more of your own ideas. Some jackets consist of lettering alone; others have a picture inside a border or may be photographic. You will need some knowledge of typography, and good

hand-drawn lettering will be a great asset, particularly for purely decorative or typographical jackets. Study your market and find a publisher using the type of cover you particularly like.

When painting book jackets I work from a base of six colours and mix intermediaries from these to give a better chance of faithful reproduction. Sometimes you may be asked to use only two or three colours, which, oddly enough, often makes the design more difficult. If you have this limitation, it is

Figs. 43a and b (below). The original jacket design for *The Holiday Which? Guide to Italy,* and the revised jacket design. The series style was altered to include the wording on a panel on the front jacket. The original artwork was returned to me to make the necessary amendments

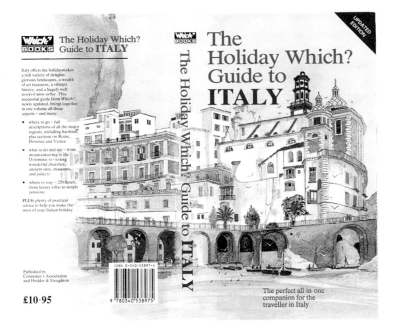

better to work in one colour and use overlays for the other colours, working in black and stating the pantone colours you wish to be used.

When preparing a folio, do include finished designs of book jackets that you have prepared, unless you have work that has already been published. If you have attended art college or a graphics course, you should have some printed samples to show, as well as the original artwork. This should always be returned by the publisher because it belongs to you, so make sure that you get original work back (unless of course you have sold it), as well as the reproduction rights. This original artwork may be very useful in obtaining future commissions.

Try some hand-drawn lettering so that you can show samples, and use type books as reference or to select typefaces for your work. You may find with some commissions, however, that a publisher or editor has his or her own ideas about lettering, or that they wish you to use an 'in-house' typeface.

You can see from the jackets illustrated in this chapter the variety that is possible, even in a specialized field. Some designs may be wholly the work of the illustrator; others may have a drawing that has been framed in a panel or panels, sometimes of the artist's design, sometimes of the art editor's. Other jackets are wrap-arounds, some are front and spine only and others have a different drawing or design on the back cover.

One of the most interesting and rewarding consequences of designing book jackets is meeting the authors. I particularly remember meeting Ethel Mannin when she was an old lady living in Devon, and she wrote to me saying how much she liked the jacket I had done of her book about Venice. Another traveller whom I met was Dervla Murphy, and I designed the jackets for several of her books. I was also fortunate to design jackets and illustrate many of Hilary Rubinstein's *Good Hotel* guides, which enabled me to visit some excellent hotels!

Fig. 44 Colour-artwork jacket design for *Drawing and Painting Architecture* (published by Van Nostrand Reinhold)

Fig. 45a Crayon-rough design for another edition of *The Holiday Which? Guide to Italy*

Fig. 45b The printed jacket design

Fig. 45c The finished
artwork

Chapter seven

BOOK ILLUSTRATION

The *Concise Oxford Dictionary* defines illustration as: 'Illustrating, drawing etc in a book. To make clear by examples or drawings; adorn with pictures'. Well, that is where we start: drawing is to create a two-dimensional image of what the writer is trying to describe with words.

At the top end of the illustrated-book market, such as folio books, the illustrations are of considerably greater value to the buyer than the text, and this can also be true of books for the private press. Illustrations for instruction and teaching manuals are of primary importance, as are those for children's books, where the artist can let himself go and give his imagination full rein. This is particularly true of the younger end of the market where the books are intended for children who cannot read or are learning to do so. Book illustration clearly has many facets, with, from my experience, the adult or older-children's books perhaps being the most difficult to illustrate. There are, in addition, other important issues to contend with, such as the look of the page, the relationship of the image to the limit of the page and the typography. As well as getting across the sense, the drawing has to decorate and enhance the text, paragraphs and headings, and the space that is left is just as important as the space used.

You may think that all this is the work of the typographer and book designer. In my view, both they and the artist should work together, although, unhappily, this is not usually the case. I know something of typography and book design, even though we live in a world of specialization where the knowledge needed has to be divided between those who are best in their own particular fields. Only perhaps in the realm of the private press is one person able to tackle the whole, and in such cases time is of lesser importance than with most book-illustration work, where the illustrator is probably brought in last and given a deadline of so many weeks or a month or two at the most. If you are offered a book to illustrate, you should try if possible to work closely with the author. I have illustrated books where I have never met the author, but first-hand discussion of ideas always proves extremely useful.

The illustrations in this chapter come from books that I have illustrated. These cover the range of my own experience, which — apart from humorous and decorative illustration — includes architecture, topography, instruction books, adventure stories and travel. All illustrators will specialize to some extent, and with experience you will learn which way you wish your work to go.

Fig. 46 Pen drawing of Lucca from the Torre Guinigi tower, reproduced in *Sketching with Ray Evans* (published by HarperCollins)

LUCCA from the Torre Guinigi.

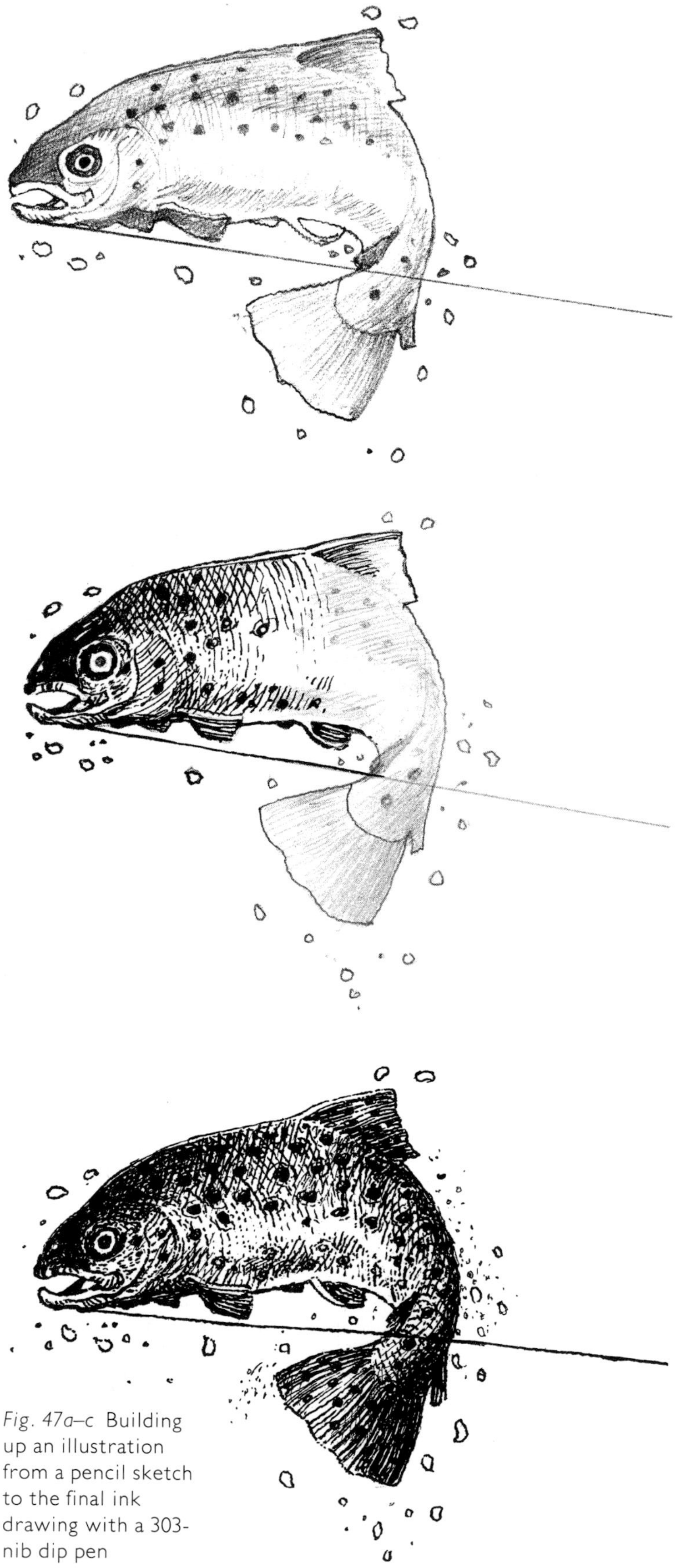

Each book has dictated a different approach, and although each has the stamp of myself as the illustrator, I have adapted my drawing to suit the type of book and its subject. Fig. 47a–c shows the method used in building up a drawing from an initial pencil sketch to the finished ink drawing ready for reproduction, although some of my travel and architectural drawings have been drawn directly in ink to keep the freshness and liveliness intact. Story illustrations, in contrast, are worked out in pencil first, either on detail paper before being trans-traced on to the paper, or drawn directly in pencil and then inked in.

PAPER

First we must choose the paper. In the past I used mainly CS Fashion board for book illustration, but with today's printing processes it is preferable to work on flexible paper or card. I like a hard surface which has a little bite, as I find a smooth paper too slippery. Some artists prefer a smooth, hard surface such as Bristol board. The work shown for *The Lighthouse Boy* and *A Childhood in Scotland* (Figs. 48 and 49) were carried out on CS10 boards, from which photographic plates were made. I never use board for colour work, because modern colour printing demands flexible paper, although it is usually possible to strip the paper off a board if necessary with the aid of a hairdryer (Fig. 50).

A Childhood in Scotland was illustrated in a decorative style. This was what was appropriate for this true story of a Scottish childhood, using my imagination together with the author's descriptions and memory, as well as photographic reference supplied by the author. The drawings for *The Lighthouse Boy* were my interpretation of

Fig. 47a–c Building up an illustration from a pencil sketch to the final ink drawing with a 303-nib dip pen

Fig. 48 Pen-and-ink illustration for *The Lighthouse Boy* (published by John Murray)

Fig. 49 Pen-and-ink drawing of a clock used in *A Childhood in Scotland*

Fig. 50 A hairdryer has many uses in the studio, including the easy removal of masking tape

that wonderful adventure story. I had to find my own reference for the costume, ships and lighthouse, and it was an enjoyable story to illustrate. I find this sort of work one of the most rewarding areas of illustration because of the opportunity it provides for imaginative input and interpretation.

CHOOSING A NIB

I have discussed this earlier (see pages 16–17), so I will just repeat that the nib you choose is a matter of personal preference. Remember, however, that it is better to draw a little larger with a broader nib than to use a finer mapping pen that may be scratchy. You will only find a nib that really suits you by trial and error.

INK

Any black Indian ink will do for book illustration, but do buy an ink with a good trade name which will be consistent and reliable. It is important that any ink you use must be waterproof.

Fig. 51 Scraperboard illustration for the children's adventure story *Rivals at Three Pines*

SCRAPERBOARD

The adventure-story-book illustration in Fig. 51 was drawn on scraperboard, which is ideal for rather stark black-and-white work and is reminiscent of wood engraving. There are different surfaces available for scraperboard, and the one I chose for these drawings was a white board, with the drawings made in pen and ink as in a normal pen drawing. If you prefer, a pencil drawing can be made first and filled in with a brush and/or pen. White lines or hatching can then be engraved into the black drawing with a scraper tool, and further drawing can be made.

Mistakes can be corrected easily with scraperboard and it is a fascinating medium. Boards are also available with half-tone surfaces, or as black board into which white lines can be engraved or larger areas scraped away using a broader tool.

TECHNIQUES

The illustration shown in Fig. 52 was one of many pictures used to illustrate Bible stories, and was drawn in Indian ink with a brush and dip pen. I printed these on a dyeline printer in my studio, but I did not put them through the developing fluid. These drawings were illustrating stories narrated by an actor, and a television camera panned down the drawing while I painted with a brush dipped in developer. I believe that this was a one-off idea, and it was used for many programmes. As we did about four takes in a day and then went out live, you can imagine how many prints we made, with the added complication that unless I covered the traces up, they would start to develop in the heat of the studio lights. It was all rather traumatic, but great fun too.

Fig. 52 Pen-and-ink drawings made on tracing paper to illustrate Bible stories for a children's television programme

Now for some tips on preparation for drawing. For pencil drawings such as the one shown in Fig. 53 (overleaf) I use an HB or a B lead, as you can achieve a dark enough tone with a B and these grades do not tend to smudge. All pencil work must be carried out with a very sharp pencil. Learn to sharpen to a long point with a sharp knife, or use an efficient automatic pencil sharpener.

When using Indian ink remember to keep the top on your bottle when not in use, because the ink will thicken up when exposed to the air. For this

reason I use a small bottle which I keep topped up from a large one, whose top is kept firmly on. If the ink thickens up too much and will not flow smoothly from the nib, add a drop of distilled water (or, if you are in the field, a drop of ordinary water), but be careful not to add too much or the ink will lose its waterproof quality.

Keep a knife handy to clean your pen nib frequently, as it will tend to clog after a great deal of drawing. Once a nib has sprung even slightly, throw it away and take a new one. Before starting with a new nib, soak it for a while in water and clean off any grease or the ink may not flow smoothly.

I keep my pens and brushes in a piece of wood with holes drilled in it (see Fig. 10 on page 20) – the nibs with points down and the brushes with the handles down. This protects the nibs, and enables the brushes to retain their points undamaged. Clean both well when you have finished using them, and dry off the points of the brushes. You can keep your brushes in a jam jar (with the points up) but for obvious reasons this is dangerous with pens. With technical pens, keep the tops firmly fitted on or they will dry out and become clogged.

Keep some blotting paper handy when you are drawing, and always have a scalpel with you in case you make a blot. If you are very quick indeed and have a jar of water with you, you may be able to wash a blot out quickly. Otherwise, blot and dry the mistake thoroughly before gently picking out the faulty mark with your scalpel and a soft eraser. With great care and patience a mistake can be completely rectified in this way.

When making pen or pencil drawings in the studio I rest my hand on a clean piece of blotting paper placed below the drawing, as the hand could be slightly greasy and spoil any drawing that may extend to where your hand has been. This also means that the paper is ready to hand in case of an emergency! Remember that it is better to work from top to bottom, and from left to right if you are right-handed; right to left if you are left-handed, to prevent smudges or marks. Lastly, when undertaking book-illustration work make sure that you work to your brief, particularly the proportion and size to which your drawings will have to fit. This may sound an obvious point, but it is surprising how easily it can be overlooked!

THE FEATHERS
LEDBURY

Chapter eight

ADVERTISING, CALENDARS AND CHRISTMAS CARDS

Advertising illustration is a very specialized subject, but is probably the widest field of all. My incursion into working for large firms and advertising their products has not had much to do with the products themselves, but has been concerned mostly with architectural or landscape paintings used to advertise the firms' names on limited-edition prints, calendars and Christmas cards. Much of this work was done for printing firms, who commissioned me and then sold the resulting design to firms who put their own logo on it.

The illustration of Christmas cards is not a new idea, but there have been changes over the years. Robins and holly with a coach and horses in the snow are not as popular as they used to be, with people choosing more sophisticated and unusual designs. Today you can buy a profusion of cards for every conceivable occasion: birthdays, anniversaries, wedding invitations, good-luck and get-well-soon cards, to name but a few. Together with the rise in the number of magazines now available on every possible topic, the number of openings for the artist seems to be increasing year by year.

One point that I would stress is to keep a very careful file of all your commissions. These can be extremely useful for future reference, but odd pieces of work very easily go astray!

PRODUCT ADVERTISING

In the early years of my career I became involved with a local studio, and joined the team as a freelance artist. I carried out many commissions for this studio concerned mainly with medical advertising, including watercolour drawings for leaflets advertising indigestion remedies. These took two forms: recipe illustrations and veteran cars for collectors.

The recipe drawings (of which an example is shown in Fig. 54) were painted on a 'Not' surface. For these, I first made a careful pencil drawing, followed by a fairly free drawing. On top of that I used Indian ink with contrasting thick and thin lines and broken lines in places. For the colour work I used bright, pure-coloured inks straight from the bottle which gave a lovely transparent finish, and obtained very attractive intermediate colours by putting one primary across another. This is the great advantage of coloured inks or bright watercolour liquids, as their brilliance makes them excellent for reproduction. The fact that coloured inks are not light-fast and will fade on exposure to light does not matter when the work is intended for reproduction.

The painting of the veteran car (Fig. 55, overleaf) needed careful drawing.

Fig. 54 (opposite) Watercolour and coloured-ink illustration for a medical advertising leaflet on indigestion remedies, 1960s

Fig. 55 Gouache drawing of a veteran car, one of a series used for medical advertising

I worked in pencil first, using a tee square, an adjustable set square and a bow-spring compass. I then painted with flat gouache colours, about one third up on the size that the car was to be printed. I used a compass with colour on for the wheels and very fine brushes for the body work, and a 0·18 mm technical pen for the inked lines. The wonderful shapes of these early cars made this a very pleasurable job with its scope for decorative artwork. Remember, as always, to limit your palette for reproduction work to obtain really accurate results.

Small-scale local advertising is a very good place to start, as I found in my early days, with work such as the advertising leaflet for Solent Wine Stores shown in Fig. 56. I made this drawing on white card using black ink with a thick pen, putting in overlays of red and yellow. I then added the lettering with white letraset and the result was quite striking.

I also continued to draw water-colours of many subjects connected with medical advertising. I acted solely as an illustrator for the work, as I was not an expert on typography. In these more sophisticated days you will find that a knowledge of typography is essential if you intend to specialize in some forms of advertising, but all illustrators should familiarize themselves with typography to some degree.

Almost immediately after leaving art college I was doing reasonably well with an agent, but I realized the limitations in my knowledge of advertising procedures. My agent had a connection with an advertising agency, and I began working for them for four days a week (I was teaching on the fifth day). During this time I was brought quickly down to earth with my idealized ideas about art and artists. I learned a great deal, although most of the time I was given boring adaptations to do with a scalpel and a tin of Cow Gum, altering existing advertising slots to go into different-shaped slots in another paper or magazine. After six months, much chastened, I became a freelance again. My subsequent work in cartooning and television, and my election to the Royal Institute of Painters in Water Colours, which brought me back to my early love of painting architecture, all formed useful 'shop windows', bringing in more and more advertising work. Always remember that *any* kind of commission – even if you consider it dull or uninspiring – may pay dividends later, and that getting your work well known and building up a wide-ranging portfolio should be your main priorities.

GENERAL ADVERTISING

For the past six years I have carried out a series of limited-edition prints for BP, each subject connected to an area close to one of their large plants or office complexes. The prints are framed and presented to clients and employees at Christmas. Each year this commission takes me to such diverse places as Aix-en-Provence, Geneva, and Cleveland in the United States, and last year it was Antwerp (Fig. 57, overleaf). I was fortunate to find a café directly opposite my subject, and I spent the whole of a rainy day and the next morning in the window. The waiter got to know me and I drank innumerable cups of coffee, ate at intervals and finished with something stronger. I completed three watercolours during that time.

It was down to earth then with a commission for a brochure to advertise a hotel (Fig. 58 on page 76), on which I worked closely with the owner. The colour illustration for the cover was fairly straightforward provided I showed the main length of the building, and I chose a view of the approach to the front entrance. A small watercolour sketch of an old well alcove was used on the back of the folder, which was printed on a very attractive card with the feel of a watercolour paper, A4 size, and folded into three. The front cover, back and third side contained a map of the area. The other side of the card (which unfolded to form the inside of the brochure) proved more difficult, as the owner suggested that I should illustrate the hotel and its environs running diagonally across two columns of type. There also had to be some exaggeration here of the surrounding country, which I tried to make typical of Dorset. I produced a drawing of the coast to run along the bottom of the inside of the brochure, and further drawings for letterheads and menus – altogether a very pleasant job. Remember that it is important to do the best work you can whether you are working for a big international company or with a single private client.

There is much in the way of advertising illustration that I cannot cover here,

Fig. 56 Ink-and-watercolour advertising leaflet for a local wine store

Fig. 57 Watercolour of Antwerp commissioned as a limited-edition print by BP. Finished size approx. 9 × 13 ins

Fig. 58 Sketch of a hotel brochure for the Innsacre Hotel in Dorset

such as computer graphics, which are new and out of my experience. There is also illustration and design work in television and cinema advertising, but, again, these are not areas of illustration with which I am familiar. There are excellent books covering the fields that I have been unable to include here (see the Bibliography on page 94). My rather simpler approach is intended for those on the threshold of their careers, and I hope will provide some ideas as a useful starting point.

CALENDARS

Large organizations produce their own Christmas and New Year cards, and often their own calendars too. As a publicity venture this is common practice nationwide, and long may it continue! In addition, many firms produce calendars as they begin to celebrate centenaries and important dates in their history. I have recently designed one such calendar for a firm's 175th anniversary.

Some printing firms design and produce calendars annually (usually a whole year ahead) which they sell to firms to put their own personalized logo on the calendar and give to clients. This has become very popular, and it was in this capacity that I began to work for Royle's Publications in the

Fig. 59a (opposite) Crayon-rough design on detail paper of the Brandenburg Gate. Used as an illustration in the EEC Capital Cities calendar for 1992, printed by Royle's for Procter & Gamble. Finished size approx. 7 × 7 ins

early 1980s. A bonus resulting from this type of work is that your paintings may often be used for a secondary purpose, in which case you will receive royalties.

The Capital Cities for the European Economic Community 1992 calendar for Procter & Gamble (commissioned and printed by Royle's) was also printed as a desk calendar for their in-house use. It was an interesting commission. I had only photographic reference from their library, although I was lucky enough to have sketches and photographs of my own that I had previously taken in Madrid, Amsterdam, Brussels and Lisbon, and I was able to carry out the London illustration in situ.

The example shown (Figs. 59a and 59b, overleaf) is of the Brandenburg Gate, for which I used several photographs, adapting rather than copying them. These days, figure reference is easier in European cities, as everyone dresses in a similar way! The figures were essential to give scale to this particular composition, and indeed nearly all the illustrations for this calendar had figures in them, as that is the nature of cities. Another nice feature of the calendar was the addition of small watercolour details relevant to each city, such as a couple of wood-and-rush chairs for Greece, and a bicycle for Amsterdam.

Five years ago I was approached by a firm of printers called Allan & Bertram to produce a calendar each year using my paintings but with a certain theme. The first was Poets' Britain, the second was Royal Britain, then Explorers' Britain and for 1992 Victorian Britain. I visited chosen sites throughout the country and made paintings for each month, featuring a different place together with a small pencil drawing. I made sketches and took photographs for each month – a watercolour sketch or painting on the spot is far more

BRANDENBURG GATE

MARCH

S M T W T F S

BERLIN

'Siegessäule

Fig. 59b
Brandenburg Gate –
the finished painting

Rugby School.

3/4/90

Fig. 60a (above)
On-the-spot sketch
of Rugby School.
Finished size
approx. 9 × 9 ins

valuable than any photograph (which may give a distorted impression of depth and perspective, and flatten tone), but supplementary photographic reference can be very helpful when you come to complete your paintings in the studio. As you can see from the examples shown, I usually follow my sketches very closely. I painted all the finished watercolours in the studio at S/S as the reproduction, but the pencil drawings were somewhat reduced.

I will take you through two of these paintings, to show you how I approached this commission. First on the list was a sketch of Rugby School: a visually exciting Victorian building (Fig. 60a–b), and I was particularly pleased with the result.

I stretched a piece of watercolour paper, masking out and protecting the edges exactly as explained on page 56, before completing a drawing of the subject. I began with the colour work by laying on flat washes of pale colour – the palest colour of the subject as a whole – and proceeded with further

Fig. 60b Finished
studio painting of
Rugby School for a
Victorian Calendar
produced by Allen
& Bertram, 1992.
Finished size
approx. 10¼ × 11¾ ins

Roy Evans

Fig. 61a–c These three stages show how I composed this illustration for the *Explorers' Britain* calendar for 1992. A preliminary watercolour study of the subject, made *in situ*, and additional photographs composed into a 'montage', provided ample reference for the final painting completed in the studio

pale washes, occasionally blotting out. I try not to put too many washes one over the other, however, as, after three washes, the transparency may be lost. That is the secret of watercolour – to keep the colours clean and transparent – so the second wash should be fairly strong and determined. Between the

washes I painted the details (in the finished painting, unlike the sketch, I was working into a lightly drawn pencil background).

I work mostly with a B-grade pencil as this is easy to clean off with a soft eraser at the end. The final wash is, usually, for the shadows, and I put

these in fairly strongly although I may wash out when half- to three-quarters dry. Then, usually but not always, I pick out details with a dip pen and Indian ink, working quickly so as not to be too mechanical. The finished work should be clean and strong, depending of course on the subject.

In my sketch of Rugby School I painted directly in watercolour, deciding where the shadows were and finishing with a technical pen – the difficulty, as always, being to maintain the spontaneity of the sketch in the finished painting.

The second illustration, shown above, was for the *Explorers' Britain* calendar. The sketch on the left shows my first approach to the subject. I found that I might need more details, especially of the foreground, so I took some photographs, and when I got home I made up a photo montage of the scene (above left). Compare the sketch and the finished painting with the montage. I have been using such montages for many years, and they can be extremely helpful. The painter David Hockney has exploited this method to the full in his work.

One of the most exciting calendars I have worked on recently was the *Shop Front* calendar for the same firm of printers. I travelled all over Britain, as

Ray Evans

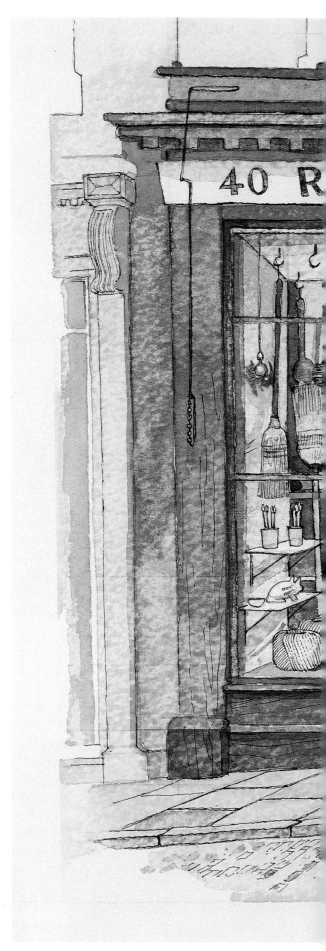

Fig. 62a–b This illustration of a brush shop in Edinburgh demonstrates the way in which I work from preliminary watercolour sketches on the spot before painting the finished artwork in the studio. I also use photographs of details that I may not have in my sketches. The finished artwork can vary from the original sketch, as happened in this case where I changed the figure in the final artwork

did the person by whom I was commissioned, until we had selected twelve of the best shop fronts that we could find. The two examples here are of a brush shop in Edinburgh (Fig. 62a–b) and a wine shop in Aldeburgh (Fig. 63a–b, overleaf). You can see the sketches that I made together with the finished studio pictures. I was lucky on both occasions with the weather; and I was pleased with the results.

I was also asked by Allan & Bertram last year to illustrate small ancillary watercolours to be used with large photographic landscapes, using flowers of the appropriate month. All these commissions came from the company seeing my work at an exhibition of the Royal Institute of Painters in Water Colours, which shows once

again how important good 'shop windows' are in obtaining work. Often you will need to be your own publicity agent as well as relying on other agencies, and building up a good portfolio with original and published work is equally important.

CHRISTMAS CARDS

These fall into a different category from calendars, and can also provide many opportunities for the illustrator.

For the Christmas card for CCA Stationery of Nelson (Fig. 64a–b, overleaf) I was asked to paint either a village street bright with decoration for Christmas, or a market scene. I chose the first option and agreed to present three crayon roughs, remembering to ask for a separate fee for the roughs. One of these was chosen (Fig. 64a), but I was asked to include more figures, enhance the decoration and add more snow. I completed the painting in watercolour and gouache, making the required adjustments, as (even if you

Fig. 63a–b This sketch of a wine shop in Aldeburgh was made on site, as with the previous illustration, and I completed the painting at home. Again, the finished artwork varied slightly from the original sketch. Both these illustrations were used in a 'Shop-front' calendar for Allen & Bertram, for 1993

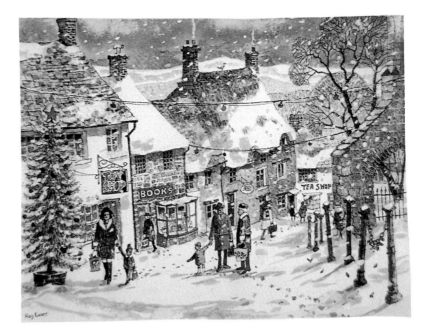

Fig. 64a (left) Colour-crayon rough for a festive-street-scene Christmas-card design for CCA printers

disagree!) it is the client who is paying the bill, and you must be flexible in your approach. The value of submitting finished, detailed roughs can also be seen here, as amendments to the actual painting would entail a great deal more work on your part, instead of putting these in at the 'rough' stage. A sketchy or inadequate rough may even lose you the job altogether if the client is dissatisfied.

A nice commission to paint the Institute of Directors' building in London proved more difficult than I had anticipated. This was because when I arrived the building was being repainted and I had to crawl about in a tin hat. As an illustrator you will often have to contend with such problems! The result was liked, however, and a limited-edition full-sized print, as well as the Christmas card, was also produced.

A card that I drew for the Eagle Star Insurance Group was to feature an interior of their wonderful William Kent house in London (see overleaf). I was rather horrified when I first saw it, as it was certainly beautiful, but the detail of the ceiling, wallpapers and carpets posed a real problem. However,

Fig. 64b (above) For the finished design, painted in watercolour and gouache, I included more figures, Christmas decorations and snow, as requested by the client

I sat on a chair for a couple of hours and the resulting sketch is shown in Fig. 65a. I was asked to make the scene suitable for Christmas, so a tree and some holly were included (such requests, as I have already mentioned, must be agreed to but with some discussion). Prior to the main sketch I had made three quick compositional sketches (one of which is shown in Fig. 65b) for the clients, who, together with the printer, were with me at this first meeting. The reason for this was to show how I meant to tackle the illustration, and, fortunately, they chose the composition that I preferred. The card itself (Fig. 65c) was painted in the studio using the sketch and photographs for detailed reference. The original was slightly larger than the reproduced size. Eagle Star subsequently decided that they needed a design on the reverse of the card, and I drew a watercolour of their eagle outside the entrance to the building.

The Royle's Publications' Christmas card for 1991 (Fig. 66b, overleaf) had to be designed to fit a large, long format, with the design extending across the front and back, and I decided on a design that included the most important buildings on the bank of the Thames, from the Tate Gallery to Tower Bridge. My crayon rough (Fig. 66a, overleaf) showed this London scene being transformed from sunset on the left to night on the right. The rough was approved in principle, but I was asked to show London at night right across the picture, rather than with the changing light.

Working S/S, I painted the finished picture from my rough, changing the sky to night throughout and substituting a Christmas tree (the firm's idea) for the entrance to London Bridge (centre right). A screen of snowflakes (not shown on the finished artwork) was finally placed over the face of the card before it was printed.

Fig. 65a (right) One of three preliminary sketches made for a Christmas card commissioned by the Eagle Star Insurance Group, featuring their splendid William Kent house in London

Fig. 65b (above) The finished rough

Fig. 65c (opposite) The finished card, complete with tree and holly, was carried out in my studio using the sketch and photographic reference

A final word of advice for this chapter. When you sign commission contracts for calendars or cards, make sure that if you sell world rights it is only for that specific use. My London Christmas card, for instance, has been sold to another company, which means that I will receive further royalties for its use. Better still, if you can sell the work just for the one purpose, then do so at the earliest stage when you are discussing prices. You must pay attention to the business aspect of being self-employed and keep proper accounts for the tax inspector. When you are established you should register for tax under Schedule D, so that you can claim adequate expenses. A pension fund for the future is also an important consideration.

Some of the work shown in Chapter Four, under editorial illustration, also comes into the category of advertising illustration, and you can see what a wide area is covered by the subject. An artist has limited time, however, and you will discover that there will be restrictions on the fields in which you can work. Like me, you will eventually specialize in certain directions, and I hope that my experience has helped to clarify some of your thoughts and intentions.

Seize every opportunity, leaving no door unopened, build up a good portfolio, treat every commission as equally important, and, with hard work, you will find that illustration becomes more than a career – it is a wonderful way of life.

Fig. 66a (left) My crayon-rough design for the Royle's Publications company Christmas card for 1992, showing the most important buildings on the bank of the Thames from the Tate Gallery to Tower Bridge

Fig. 66b (below) For the finished painting, the artwork was changed to depict a night scene right across the design. A Christmas tree was also introduced, and a snow screen was subsequently printed over the card

BIBLIOGRAPHY

AUSTEN, JOHN *The ABC of Pen and Ink Rendering* (Isaac Pitman, 1937)

BORGMAN, HARRY *Drawing in Ink* (Watson-Guptill, 1977)

BRIDGEWATER, PETER *An Introduction to Graphic Design* (Apple Press Ltd, 1987)

CAMPBELL, ALISTAIR *The Designer's Handbook* (Macdonald, 1983)

COOK, BRIAN *The Britain of Brian Cook: A Batsford Heritage* (Batsford, 1987)

DALLEY, TERENCE (ed.) *The Complete Guide to Illustration and Design* (Phaidon, 1984)

DAVIES, RUSSELL *Ronald Searle* (Sinclair-Stevenson, 1990)

HOAR, FRANK *Pen and Ink Drawing* (Acanthus, 1955)

HOFFPAUIR, STEPHAN & ROSNER, JOYCE *Architectural Illustration in Watercolour* (Whitney Library of Design, 1989)

HOGARTH, PAUL *Drawing Architecture* (Pitman, 1973)

JENNINGS, SIMON (ed.) *Professional Illustration and Design* (Quarto, 1987)

KLEMIN, DIANA *The Illustrated Book* (Bramhall House, New York, 1965)

MARTIN, JUDY & STEAR, GEOFF *Studio Tips and Tricks* (Outline Press, 1989)

SMITH, STAN *Anatomy, Perspective and Composition* (Macdonald, 1984)

SMITH, STAN & TEN HOLT, PROFESSOR F. (eds.) *The Artist's Manual* (Macdonald, 1980)

SZABO, MARC *Drawing File for Architects, Illustrators and Designers* (Van Nostrand Reinhold, 1976)

The Illustrated Figure Reference Manual (Bloomsbury, 1987)

THELWELL, NORMAN *Wrestling with a Pencil* (Methuen, 1986)

WILLIS, JIM & JANET *The Art of Frank Patterson* (Cyclists' Touring Club, 1979)

Writers' & Artists' Yearbook (A & C Black, annual publication)

FURTHER READING

EVANS, RAY *Drawing and Painting Architecture* (Van Nostrand Reinhold, 1983)

EVANS, RAY *Drawing and Painting Buildings* (HarperCollins, 1989)

GLASHAN, JOHN *John Glashan's World* (Robinson Publishing, 1991)

HARRISON, HAZEL *Houses and Buildings* (Studio Vista, 1992)

MARTIN, JUDY *Encyclopaedia of Coloured Pencil Techniques* (Quarto, 1992)

MARTIN, JUDY *Sketching* (HarperCollins, 1991)

INDEX